ANN MAINSE

D1739108

Coffee with Him

MORNINGS WITH **GOD** ON AN UNEXPECTED JOURNEY

For Amanda,
God bless you!
Ann Mainse
Isaiah 36:3

A **31-DAY** DEVOTIONAL
VOLUME 1

Scripture Quotations

ISBN: 9798639856730

First printing, 2020

Contact c/o
Heart to Heart Marriage & Family Ministries
1295 North Service Road
Burlington, Ontario, Canada
L7R 4M2

For more information, visit www.aBetterUs.tv

Thank you to our dear friend and amazing recording
artist/worship leader, Dan Macaulay, for his
creativity, expertise, and especially his patience in
designing the cover and layout of this book
(danmac.org).

This picture was taken during round six of my eight chemo sessions. Ron was by my side for every single one.

… to have and to hold,

for better for worse,

for richer for poorer,

to love and to cherish,

in sickness and in health…

Two college kids spoke those vows 36 years ago,
thinking we knew exactly what they meant.
Little did we know how little did we know.

And yet, over the years we indeed held each other
through the better and the worse,
and now, more recently, through the sickness.
And I have felt loved and cherished beyond
measure.

This book is lovingly dedicated to my college sweetheart,
my life partner, my heart's keeper, and the most loyal and
loving person I've ever known,
my husband, Ron.

Contents

Foreword

By Ron Mainse

"Let's hang up right now so you can write your first journal entry." Those were the words I felt strongly to say to Ann on the day she was told of her breast cancer diagnosis.

I was driving home from a charity golf tournament where I didn't make it to the first tee, because Ann had called me with the shocking results of her recent biopsy. We were shaken to the core...an experience we had felt several times before in our 35 years of married life, but now it was a lot more threatening and personal. "I'm coming home right now, and I'll call you from the car as soon as I'm on the road," I told her. Grabbing my golf bag from the cart, I told my foursome friends in vague terms that something urgent had come up and I had to leave right away.

As I fired up my GPS to begin my two-hour drive home from a place I had never been before, I was painfully aware of my inadequacy to navigate this new journey we had just begun. I quickly called Ann back and we started down the road together. We talked...we cried...we prayed...and about half-way home she said that she felt prompted to write about what she was feeling and what God had already started speaking to her heart. And that was the genesis of this book.

It has been difficult for me to see Ann, my beloved Treasure, travel down this uncharted road. I awkwardly tried to discover my support role as a husband. How could I come alongside Ann with the right sensitivity through her emotional ups and downs? As she experienced the long, drawn-out treatment process, complete with nausea, hair loss, and exhaustion, I often missed the mark in trying to strike the right balance between cheerleading and empathy. However, it seemed like what she simply needed most from me was my presence...and a loving embrace.

As I've stumbled through my role, I thank God that Ann sensed a much more significant Presence on this journey, whose loving embrace she felt daily, and whose words ALWAYS hit the mark. While I tried to be her small "r" rock, her real security for her soul was found resting in her BIG "R," her solid Rock. And knowing that Ann's main "go-to" Person was the Almighty Lord of the Universe took a lot of pressure off of this overwhelmed and inadequate husband's heavy heart.

Every morning, along with her soothing cup of coffee, Ann would spend time nestled solidly in the peaceful palm of God's loving hand...whether through a special Scripture, a dynamic devotional, a soothing song, or a poignant prayer.

As quickly as Ann would receive a download from

the heart of God, she felt compelled to upload it out to others who might be on a challenging journey of their own. Her regular social media posts quickly became a wellspring of refreshment for many weary travelers...and this book is the result of others encouraging Ann to compile her unique insights into book form. You'll find Ann's writing style to be refreshing and conversational, as she is not one to feel confined by strict rules of grammar... similar to one of her favourite authors, Max Lucado.

May you be inspired and encouraged on your journey as you join Ann in the comfort of God's presence... and share a *"Coffee with Him."*

Introduction

By Ann Mainse

I was alone in the house when the phone rang. It was my doctor. She had the results of my recent biopsy.

"I can't believe it, Ann, but cancer cells were detected."

I shook my head as if to clear my thoughts. No, that couldn't be right. She kept talking.

"I'm shocked too," she said. "You've been so faithful with your mammograms and they've always been fine. But this one was different."

My head was spinning.

She gave me more information before we hung up, and then I just sat. Stunned.

Ron was gone for the day at a golf tournament... almost 2 hours away.

Should I call him?

Should I wait until he gets home... in approximately 10 hours?

Should I give him one last day to be normal... before his life changes forever?

Finally, I decided to call him, just to see how he was doing. I would decide what to do from there.

"Hi Honey! I think I may have just won the putting competition!" He laughed as he said those words and my heart sank. I was so tempted not to tell him. To let him enjoy his day. But then I wondered what he would want. And I had my answer.

After asking Ron if he could slip away somewhere private where we could talk, I broke the news to him. He immediately said he was coming home and that he would call me from the car.

During his first hour of driving we talked and cried and prayed and cried some more. Him stuck in traffic and me alone at home.

At one point I said to Ron that I felt God wanted me to journal my journey, to write down what my heart is processing through the lens of God's grace. I couldn't explain it. I just knew I had to.

That's when Ron said to me, "I'll be home in about 45 minutes. Let's hang up and you take this time to write your first journal entry."

And so I did.

By the time Ron got home, I had my first entry written.

Over the course of the next several months I often felt the need to write. And many times I sensed God's compassionate Spirit guide my jumbled thoughts.

After sharing a couple of my journal entries with close friends, I felt I needed to share them more broadly. *Maybe they could help others*, I thought.

And so it began.

Every morning I would post on Facebook a Scripture that God had used in my heart that day and a devotional thought to go with it. And before I knew it, thousands began tracking with me, many encouraging me to put these posts into a book. The book you're holding in your hands is the result of that encouragement.

I have included many of my Facebook posts, as well as some devotionals that felt too personal to share on a public forum.

At the end of each reading, you will find some "Sips to Savour"… a couple of questions to encourage your personal reflection. As well, I have suggested a "Prayer Starter"… a line or two that you might use to begin a conversation with the Lord. You will also find a "Notes" area with blank lines where You can jot down your thoughts…what you feel God may be speaking to your heart.

At the back of the book, I have included a treasury of "Meaningful Scriptures to Percolate On" (to continue our coffee theme ☺)... precious gems from God's Word that have meant a lot to me during my unexpected journey. I encourage you to focus on one or two of these Scriptures each day, even printing them out and placing them around the house, as I often did. Several of them found a home in my bedroom, on my bathroom mirror, on the fridge door and other places.

It is my prayer that no matter where you find yourself today, whether on a breath-stealing, terrifying journey, or simply navigating the twists and turns of everyday life, that you will find your strength in God.

So for the next 31 days, grab a mug, find a comfy spot, and join me as we receive hope and healing from the One Who loves us most... and share a *"Coffee with Him."*

What do I do?

Be still, and know that I am God!
I will be honored by every nation.
I will be honored throughout the world.
Psalm 46:10 (NLT)

NOTE: This first journal entry was written on June 10, 2019... the day my new journey began.

"What do I do, Lord? I DON'T KNOW WHAT TO DO!" Those were the sobs I heard coming from my own lips. Panicked. Tearful. Fearful. The words just kept coming. Repeating. Assaulting. "I DON'T KNOW WHAT TO DO! I DON'T KNOW WHAT TO DO!" It was like my senses were in a free-fall, my arms flailing in mid-air. All alone I began pacing through the house. Crying. Praying. Pleading. This was frightening, unknown territory and, well, I just needed an answer.

And that's when I saw it. It was on the wall near our front door... artwork that contains four words. Four short words. And I was drawn to them like a magnet.

be still and know

Oh, those four comforting words from Psalm 46... a calming reminder to be still and know that HE is God. And a calming reminder was exactly what I needed.

> *Oh, those four comforting words from Psalm 46... a calming reminder to be still and know that HE is God.*

"You have breast cancer." Those were the words my doctor just told me over the phone. Four more words. Now at this point it might seem like I'm kind of burying the lead. I mean, isn't that the headline? I guess on the surface you might think so. But, to be honest, I'm not feeling very "surface" right now. Because as devastating and scary and threatening as those four words are, they ultimately drove me to those *other* four words. And believe it or not, they ARE "the lead."

Be still and know... that HE is in control.

Be still and know... that HE will never leave me.

Be still and know... that HE cares intimately.

Be still and know... that HE is God.

And while I have SO MANY questions about so many things... today... for now... at the very beginning of this unexpected journey... I CHOOSE to focus on what I do know. On what I can do.

Be still and know that HE is God.

♡ What am I anxious about today that's brimming with unanswered questions?

♡ How can I "be still" today to receive God's peace?

Heavenly Father, I lift up my fears and worries to You, knowing that You will replace them with Your Peace that "passes all understanding" (Phil. 4:7). I am still as I rest securely in the palm of Your hand, knowing YOU ARE GOD, and You love me.

Notes

A Thoughtful Battle
(Part One)

Take every thought captive...
2 Corinthians 10:5 (NIV)

Since my world was literally turned upside down three days ago with the cancer diagnosis, I've been in a battle. A thought-provoking battle. A sleep-stealing, joy-sucking, peace-obliterating battle. And it's been raging. And I've been scared. And as I've contemplated this battle, my mind began to wander...

Those medieval times movies... you know the ones. Where there are lots of swords and horses and knights and armour. And battlefield scenes. LOTS of battlefield scenes.

You know who the good guys are but when the swords start flying (and the bodies start falling) it's kind of hard to find them. To track their progress. They're fighting for a good cause and you hope that the writers will use the battle to advance their efforts. But the struggle goes on. And on. [Ok, personally, I've found those battle scenes go on a little too long for my liking. Enough already!] But, finally, the battle does come to an end. And we're happy to see that most of the good guys are still standing, albeit bloodied and beaten.

*Those scary...
obtrusive...
fear-inducing
thoughts
ONLY have
power over
me IF I give
it to them.*

So.... what in the world does any of this have to do with taking every thought captive? Good question. I guess it's just how my mind works.

Since June 10, the day of my breast cancer diagnosis, my mind has been in a battle. And while there are no horses or armour, the battle has raged just the same.

My opponents? Thoughts. *What will the CT scan reveal? What will the doctors tell me? Will I be here for the birth of my next grandchild? Will I grow old with my husband?* Terrifying, random scenarios that may or may not happen.

Thoughts. Sword-wielding, evil-intending, unrelenting thoughts. And over the last few days I have mistakenly pictured myself fighting them. Bloodied and beaten, I've been doing my best to take them captive... but finding the battle raging just a little too long for my liking.

Until I read that verse again (this time without Hollywood's imagery behind it). I wanted to see that verse more clearly. No, I *NEEDED* to see that verse more clearly. And, this time, the battle looked entirely different.

Take. Every. Thought. Captive.

Hmmm... Ok. Simple. Straight-forward.

And maybe I'm finally beginning to realize that the thoughts I'm battling actually DON'T have swords. In fact, they don't have any power at all. Those scary... obtrusive... fear-inducing thoughts ONLY have power over me IF I give it to them.

[Cue my "ah-ha moment"]

Picturing them as intimidating, iron-clad warriors was giving them the power to be something they're not. They are NOT Goliath-sized opponents. They are NOT towering over me, matching my blade, thrust for thrust.

While scary, yes, they are actually more like novels I choose to read than they are opponents I must defeat.

And that epiphany has made all the difference. *Take every thought captive...*

Take every lingering fear... every wanna-be-rabbit-trail... every twinge of uncertainty... captive. Take away the sword. Take away the fear. Take away their power.

And put those fictional novels back on the shelf... where they belong.

Sips to Savour

♡ What thoughts am I doing battle with today? ... and who seems to be winning?

♡ Have I allowed fearful thoughts to have power that does not belong to them?

♡ How can I adopt a completely new mindset in dealing with my mental foes, following the Bible's directive to "take every thought captive"?

Prayer Starter

Help me, dear Lord, to do battle in my thought life today, fortified with Your armour (Ephesians 6:10-17). I take not only a defensive posture, but help me to also go on the offensive with Your powerful "Sword of the Spirit," which is Your Word... the Bible.

Notes

Day 3

A Thoughtful Battle (Part Two)

Take every thought captive...
2 Corinthians 10:5 (NIV)

I'm amazed at the patience of God.
I mean, really.

He so lovingly gives us an inspiration... a flash of wisdom... an insight into HIS heart... and we breathe a sigh of relief as all is right in our world.

But then without fail, fear creeps in. And before you know it, our head overrules our heart... and our heart is once again in turmoil.

I'm ashamed to say it... but that was me not too long ago.

[Cue the patience of God.]

You may have noticed that in my previous journal entry I had successfully discovered how to "take every thought captive."

And so I did.

And then more time went by. And with it, my peace.

[Sigh]

Hence the need for "Part Two" today...

My thoughts have swords.

There. I said it.

I know I had an epiphany. I truly believe that God's Holy Spirit spoke to my spirit, helping me to re-align my thinking... about my thoughts.

And it's all still true.

But as I continue to wait to see the doctor (any doctor) to find out more about my cancer diagnosis (other than the fact that this is my diagnosis), my thoughts have run rampant. My breath is taken away at the rabbit trails... the what-ifs... the worst-case scenarios.

My inner dialogue is once again on overdrive.

Argh!!!

To be totally honest, I usually don't see it coming. It's when I least expect it that there's a subtle tap on my shoulder and a menacing whisper in my ear, and I turn just in time to see the flash of a sword.

And fear has the battle raging once more.

And the heaviness returns. And the dread is overwhelming.

And that's when I have a choice to make.

I have to choose to take action... to step right up and grab fear's sword. With more courage than my feeble heart possesses, I have to gird myself in GOD'S armour, open my heart to His strength, and stand eye-to-eye with the enemy, commanding it to bow in the presence of God's mighty power.

He so lovingly gives us an inspiration... a flash of wisdom... an insight into HIS heart... and we breathe a sigh of relief as all is right in our world.

And while I don't totally understand it (ok, I don't even remotely understand it), I do know one thing. It works. As I submit my thoughts to Him and allow God's Spirit to renew my mind, the tide of the battle turns.

In the presence of my all-loving, all-powerful, all-encompassing God, fear doesn't stand a chance.

It must bow.

And I am relieved. And I can rest.

But... I must remember.

Because as sure as the sun will rise tomorrow, I know for a fact that fear will too. Sometime soon, I'll feel that familiar tap on my shoulder, hear that menacing whisper in my ear.

But this time it will be different.

Will my breath be taken away? Yes. Will I have a choice to make? Yes.

And my choice will be this... This time I'll let God's Spirit IN ME answer the call.

I'll let HIM face down the fear.

And then... when fear comes knocking once more...

... I'll let Him do it again.

Sips to Savour

♡ Is my mind racing today with "what ifs" and worst-case scenarios?

♡ How do I usually respond to fear's menacing whisper?

♡ How can I let God's Spirit in me answer the enemy's tap on my shoulder?

Prayer Starter

Lord God, when the battle in my mind starts to rage, I will choose to let You and Your Truth do the fighting. And I will rest in Your perfect love, which Your Word says "casts out all fear" (1 John 4:18).

Notes

_____

_____

_____

_____

_____

_____

_____

_____

The Heart Guard

...and the peace of God, which surpasses all understanding, will guard your hearts and minds through Christ Jesus.
Philippians 4:7 (NKJV)

Today is the day. I am seeing the surgeon. I will finally get some answers.

And I'm nervous.

For the last eight days the only information I've had is my diagnosis of a particular form of breast cancer. "If you're going to Google it," my doctor said over the phone, "only go on the Mayo Clinic website. There's a lot of scary misinformation out there that you don't need to worry about."

Now that's comforting.

And so for the past eight days, on the Mayo Clinic

website, I have read and re-read all I could on my diagnosis, firmly resisting the urge to walk through the many other dark doors that Mr. Google is offering before me.

Nope. Not going there.

I know who's lurking just over that threshold... and FEAR is not invited on this journey.

"Be anxious for nothing, but in everything by prayer and petition, with thanksgiving, let your requests be made known to God. And the peace of God, which surpasses all understanding, will guard your hearts and minds in Christ Jesus."
(Philippians 4:6-7)

Immediately my heart recited those words.

I discovered the verses from Philippians when our kids were young. Ron was commuting to and from work three hours a day, and I was babysitting children in our home (along with taking care of my own) just to make ends meet. And most of the time, they weren't meeting. To say finances were tight was an understatement, and I felt its constrictive pressure constantly.

I remember one night after the kids were in bed and Ron was working late, I was standing in the kitchen, alone, crying out to God. I knew I needed something. I knew I needed the divine.

And that's when I stumbled upon these verses. I wrote them down and put them on the fridge door. And over the next few days, with every trip to fill a bottle... or make a snack... or get one more cup of juice for the kids... I made a point of reading those words and committing them to memory.

I knew I needed them. I was *desperate* for peace.

Sometimes the peace we need isn't a passive one, like a minister would convey to his parishioners... "Peace be unto you." Sometimes we need an *authoritative* peace, the kind that Jesus commanded on the sea... "PEACE, BE STILL!"

> *Sometimes we need an authoritative peace, the kind that Jesus commanded on the sea... "PEACE, BE STILL!"*

Sometimes we need Jesus to step into our storm and **remind it of just Who is Boss.**

It's a powerful peace... guarding our heart, protecting our mind.

It's an encouraging peace... reminding us, over and over, that we are not alone.

And it's a transcending peace... reassuring us that the One greater than the storm is STILL in control.

It's a peace... *which surpasses all understanding.*

And as I begin, in earnest, my journey through this current storm, the offshoot of that Truth becomes my lifeline.

Because no matter what the doctor says today, I choose to walk in HIS peace.

Sips to Savour

♡ What storm is raging within me that needs to be stilled by "The Boss"... the Prince of Peace?

♡ Do I have items on my worry list that need to be turned into a prayer list, in line with Philippians 4:6-7?

Prayer Starter

Lord God, I want to do as Your Word tells me, so I give You my anxious thoughts today as I lift up my requests to You in prayer. I receive the promise of Your peace that will guard my heart and mind... an amazing peace beyond my understanding!

Notes

A Divine Conversation

He will take delight in you with gladness.
With His love, He will calm all your fears.
He will rejoice over you with joyful songs.
Zephaniah 3:17 (NLT)

Waiting is so hard. When I was little, waiting for something good, like Christmas morning, was as close to torture as my young mind could imagine. Now that I'm older and the outcome isn't guaranteed as "good," my imagination is truly the purveyor of my torture.

It's been two weeks since my breast cancer diagnosis. Two tumultuous weeks. Two weeks of shock... numbness... fear... uncertainty.

Two weeks of wearisome nights, needing to find rest in the midst of the storm. But also two weeks of quiet early mornings... drawn by His precious Spirit to a secret place of solitude and peace.

And as I have discovered... therein lies the gift.

For if the long, wearisome nights conjure memories of my childhood "torture," then the sunrise secret place is my Christmas morning. Because it's in that place where He speaks.

Oh, He always invites me to speak first... and more times than not, I do. And then... a heartbeat later... with the warmth and understanding of an oh-so-patient Father, He answers.

I say...

It's me again, Lord. You must be so tired of hearing about my fears and worries. I'm sorry I'm such a bother, but I don't know where else to turn.

And He whispers...

Oh My child, I rejoice over you! My heart sings at the beauty of you. Rest with Me awhile and let Me quiet you with my love.
Zephaniah 3:17

I say...

But God, I'm scared and I don't know what to do.

He whispers...

Hold tightly to Me, for I have promised to never leave you and I am reliable and trust-

worthy and faithful to My word...
Hebrews 10:23-24

I say...

I've never faced anything like this before... I don't understand what's happening.

And He whispers...

You are safe with Me, for My power is great and absolute. My understanding is unlimited. Psalm 147:5

I say...

But what if the road ahead is terrifying?

And He whispers...

> *For if the long, wearisome nights conjure memories of my childhood "torture," then the sunrise secret place is my Christmas morning. Because it's in that place where He speaks.*

When you walk through difficult times, I will be with you. I will take care of you. I guarantee it.
Isaiah 43:2

I say...

But I'm scared...

And He whispers...

Give to Me all your worries and concerns and I will carry them. 1 Peter 5:7 **I will never leave you nor forsake you.** Deuteronomy 31:6

And I say...

Sometimes my thoughts feel overwhelming...

And He whispers...

Take every thought captive under My authority. 1 Corinthians 5:10 **Be transformed by the renewing of your mind.** Romans 12:2

I say...

Renew my mind? It's too hard.

So, God whispers...

Let Me make your thoughts and words pure and acceptable in My sight. Psalm 19:14

And then, timidly, I say...

Sometimes I feel so alone...

And God whispers...

Nothing can separate you from My love... neither your fears for today nor your worries about tomorrow...
Romans 8:38

I say...

... still sometimes I'm afraid.

And He whispers...

**You don't have to be afraid. I am with you.
I am your God. I will make you strong and
help you. I will hold you safe in My hands.**
Isaiah 41:10

And I say...

*My fears... my tears... my worries. Sometimes I feel
unworthy of Your love.*

And He gently smiles and says...

**I have loved you with an everlasting love...
I have watched you since before you were
born... I've heard every prayer, kept every
tear... You are precious in My sight.** Jeremiah 31:3, Psalm 139:15, 16; 56:8, 1 Peter 3:4

And finally, I say...

*In this quiet place, tell my heart what it needs most
to hear. I am listening.*
And lovingly He whispers...

Be still and KNOW that I am God. Psalm 46:10
Over these last two weeks on this rollercoaster of
emotions, I think I've learned something. In the

midst of all of my tortuous imaginings, the numbness, the fear, the uncertainty... in the middle of it all... lies my secret place.

It's only a breath away.

And it is in *that* place where He speaks.

And I am at peace.

Sips to Savour

♡ Have I spent time in that "secret place" with God today where I can enter into a "divine conversation" with Him?

♡ What do I hear God whispering to my heart in answer to my fears and struggles?

Prayer Starter

Thank You, Lord God, that You are with me in my journey and tenderly speak Your loving Truth to my heart when I need it most. May I keep returning to that secret place with You.

Notes

_____

_____

_____

_____

_____

_____

_____

_____

_____

_____

_____

_____

_____

_____

_____

_____

_____

_____

_____

_____

_____

Day 6

Weepy Day

...You have collected all my tears
in Your bottle...
Psalm 56:8 (NLT)

It's a weepy day. Tears are coming easily today... and flowing freely. Not sobs. Not ugly cries. Just tears. Leaky, unpredictable tears.

Surgery is just under a month away and, today, the small circle of people who know of my breast cancer diagnosis has enlarged significantly.   As it should. I firmly believe in the power of prayer and to let a larger number of friends and acquaintances know of my situation... only makes sense.

Yet, in some strange way, today, I feel like *I'm* finding out for the first time. Again. And it hurts.

It's a weepy day. My tears are flowing freely.

I wonder how God feels about that.

I mean, He knows I love Him. He knows I trust Him. He knows that my heart's anchor is firmly rooted in His faithfulness. And He sees my tears.

I know He does.

> *He knows that my heart's anchor is firmly rooted in His faithfulness. And He sees my tears.*

And yet... I feel absolutely no condemnation.

Because the Face that my watery eyes look into... is smiling. And tender. And loving. And I think maybe... just maybe... is a little tear-stained too.

And that makes me smile.

Because, in my heart, I know that my sorrow is just as precious to Him as my joy. It's the deepest part of me. It's part of who I am. And in His oh-so-gentle way, He waits. He's not trying to rush me through it. In fact, He's already told me in His Word that instead of discouraging my tears, He's been collecting them.

And I love that.

Because today's a weepy day. And on this day, it seems all I can do is give Him more.

And He smiles.

> *"You keep track of all my sorrows. You have collected all my tears in Your bottle. You have recorded each one in Your book."*
> Psalm 56:8 (NLT)

Sips to Savour

♡ Have I ever felt self-condemnation for my tears, like it was somehow a lack of faith and trust in God?

♡ Even in the midst of my tears, how can I rest in God's presence today and look into His loving, smiling Face?

Prayer Starter

Thank You, Lord God, for understanding my frail human emotions and still loving me so patiently. Just knowing You're with me in my distress is such sweet comfort. In Your gentle presence I am free to expose the deepest part of me without condemnation.

Notes

Joy in the Storm

It is the LORD who goes before you. He will be with you; He will not leave you or forsake you. Do not fear or be dismayed.
Deuteronomy 31:8 (AMP)

Prince Edward Island is *beautiful*. Ron and I flew in a couple of days ago to celebrate our 35th wedding anniversary. It's a trip we had meticulously planned 6 months ago… before our worlds were turned upside down with this unexpected journey.

Before cancer.

With all that was changing in our world, I wasn't even sure it was a good idea. With my mind so pre-occupied with adjusting schedules, doctor's appointments and finger-tip information, would the purpose of the trip be wasted on me?

Yet Ron insisted we go. And we did.

Prince Edward Island is *red*.

As our plane descended through the stormy (turbu-
lence-inducing) clouds, I got my first glimpse. As
if sewn together with various scraps of colourful
cloth, the patchwork outside my window was varied
and vibrant and stunning. And as we rented a car
and drove through the countryside, the beauty only
deepened.

Vast forested hills... colourful seaside cottages...
wildflower-lined roads. The many hues and textures
vied for my attention, and all I could do was sit and
soak it all in.

And for several glorious minutes there was no cancer. No surgery. No unknown.

And I could breathe.

However, by the time we reached our Bed & Break-
fast in Cavendish... the anticipated storm had begun.
And it was raging. Strong winds and heavy rain
demanded we dash onto the spacious front porch,
through the blossoming garden, past the inviting
porch swing. The open front door our only focus.

It's funny how storms do that. They demand all of
our attention, causing us to miss blessings that are
all around us.

I mean really.

The beauty in our lives is just as real when the skies are gray as when they are blue... yet, during a storm, we don't seem to notice. It's the sudden change in our surroundings that draws our attention... and keeps it laser-locked, away from the blessings.

Prince Edward Island is *wet*.

We're now into our third day on the island and the rain has barely stopped. But that's ok. Because something has changed.

It's funny how storms do that. They demand all of our attention, causing us to miss blessings that are all around us.

For even though we have yet to see a blue sky, the gardens are oh-so-lovely. And even though a heavy mist has blanketed the air, we have chosen to walk instead of run... to soak in the sights (even as we are getting soaked ourselves)... to no longer dash through the glories of this majestic place. And even though we may get wind-blown and battered, we have decided to enjoy the journey.

Hmmm...

To slow down. To notice the beauty. To find joy in the storm.

What a brilliant insight for all of the unexpected journeys in our life.

Maybe that's the purpose of this trip after all.

∼ Sips to Savour ∼

♡ What beauty or blessings around me might I be missing due to a storm that seems to demand all my attention?

♡ How can I cut through today's dreary drizzles to see with my Father's eyes the good that He is working in me... and enjoy the journey?

∼ Prayer Starter ∼

Father God, thank You for Your presence on this journey. Help me to keep a thankful attitude and appreciate the bright blessings You have shone into my life, despite the current "weather forecast."

Notes

Surprising Tears

*He will swallow up death forever; and the
Lord God will wipe away tears from all
faces...* Isaiah 25:8 (NKJV)

When this unexpected journey began in June, I didn't know about the tears. I knew about the shock... the fear... the uncertainty. I guess I kind of anticipated the sleepless nights, finally finding peace in God's presence... and the early mornings soaking in His Word. All of those things seem to be part and parcel of this unexpected journey.

What I didn't anticipate were the tears.

They seem to be always near the surface, waiting for release.

Like a water-logged carpet, they're not really apparent until a slight pressure is applied... and then they're all encompassing.

And it doesn't take much to bring them out.

Making plans for the future. Reminiscing about the past. Appreciating blessings in the present. Dwelling for too long on any of these usually starts the waterworks.

And that's what surprises me. But maybe it shouldn't.

Because when you go through an unexpected journey like this, it touches every part of who you are. From "set-in-stone" calendar commitments... to impromptu pick-up-and-go's... to carefree days of dreaming about the future. Every part of your life is brought to a grinding halt. And there are so many questions. And the uncertainty is terrifying.

I didn't anticipate the tears.

I've never been one to easily cry. Ok, maybe I have... especially during a touching movie. I mean, who didn't cry at the end of *Marley & Me*? But usually I'm able to hold it together. To soldier on.

But not now.

And maybe that's ok.

Because sometimes leaking eyes are a by-product of a wounded heart. And it's the heart that dictates their release.

I was 9 years old when I gave my heart to Jesus. And in the decades since, He has held me close through some pretty tear-inducing times.

The death of my brother. Losing both of my parents. The deceitfulness and betrayal of a friend.

Because of God's Lordship in my life... because He has free access to every nook, every cranny of my soul... I am at peace.

All moments where my heart simply couldn't hold back. Like a torrential rain from an angry thundercloud, my tears knew no bounds.

And now there's this. Cancer. The most personal... most intimate trial I've ever faced.

And surprisingly, it's because of that fact that I'm finding the deepest level of comfort yet.

Because of God's Lordship in my life... because He has free access to every nook, every cranny of my soul... because there is nowhere in the deepest recesses of my imagination that I can go and He's NOT already there... I am at peace. And that's surprising too.

Do the tears still come?

Yes.

Is He there with me, quietly wiping them away?

Absolutely.

Does THAT surprise me?

Ahhh... No.

Sips to Savour

♡ Have there been times when my tears have surprisingly come out of nowhere?

♡ In those times, how can I posture myself in God's presence to allow Him access to every hidden area of my heart, so that His soothing presence brings a deep peace?

Prayer Starter

Lord God, thank You for Your soothing presence and peace. Today, I welcome Your healing hand to gently wipe away my tears and calm my troubled soul.

Notes

All Encompassing

David, ceremonially dressed in priest's linen,
danced with great abandon before God.
2 Samuel 6:14 (MSG)

All-encompassing. That's what it feels like. It's been over a month since my cancer diagnosis and now surgery will take place in 3 days' time.

And my new reality is all-encompassing.

From scheduling and then re-scheduling events for our ministry... to adjusting family time with our kids... to everyday decisions like what I can and cannot eat... my new reality is heart-rending.

And it's hard to *not* feel overwhelmed.

Don't eat sugar... stop drinking coffee... avoid soy at all costs... say no to bananas and pineapples and cherries... And every form of dairy... And whatever you do, definitely no red meat. I find myself daily bombarded with new well-meaning suggestions and restrictions... and the carefree life I once knew is now filed away like a distant childhood memory.

Oh, don't get me wrong. I'm all for choosing a healthier lifestyle. And some of these newfound "stay-away-froms" are probably for the better anyway. It's just that this overshadowing diagnosis has robbed me of more than simply menu selection.

It has taken my sense of abandon. It's robbed me of my joy.

You know what I mean... that childlike desire to splash around in a summer rainstorm or ride your bike through the middle of a mud puddle. It's knowing that you're probably going to get wet and dirty, but you don't care... because the exhilarating freedom is so worth it.

Healthy abandon.

And while some may consider that kind of thinking to be only for our kids, I can't help but wonder if even a little of it is good for us grown-ups too.

And that's what I miss. It's what I need. And I don't think I'm alone.

In 2 Samuel 6:14, we're told that King David *danced with great **abandon*** before God (MSG), even while wearing the "structured" ceremonial garment of a priest.

In chapter 40:3, the Psalmist celebrated the people **abandon**ing *themselves to God (MSG).*

And in 2 Corinthians 9:9, the Apostle Paul stated that even God *throws caution to the winds, giving to the needy in reckless [joyful]* **abandon** *(MSG).*

Great... celebratory... joyful... abandon.

Maybe it's not such a bad thing. Maybe it's something worth protecting.

> *While my outer world is structured and monitored and measured, my inner spirit will soar in God's grace and glory.*

And as I continue to navigate my way down unknown paths, my physical world shrinking before my eyes, this one thing I will do. I will join with the Apostle Paul when he joyfully declared in Romans chapter 5...

*"Because of Jesus... We find ourselves standing [with **abandon**] where we always hoped we might stand—out in the wide-open spaces of God's grace and glory, standing tall and shouting our praise."* Romans 5:2 (MSG)

I love that. While my outer world is structured and monitored and measured, my inner spirit will soar in

God's grace and glory.

Yep... that's what I'll do.

That's where I'll find my joy.

And along the way, maybe I'll go and find a mud puddle too.

Sips to Savour

♡ In the middle of my daily grind and structure, when was the last time I threw caution to the wind... abandoning myself in worship and obedience to God?

♡ Though I might have physical limitations, how can I break free today and allow God's sweet presence to lift my spirit to new, exhilarating heights?

Prayer Starter

Lord God, today I choose to worship You with abandon... dancing in spirit, and even in body, before You. And I am raised up to soar on wings like eagles! (Isaiah 40:31).

Notes

The Blue Folder

*... the peace of God (a peace that is beyond
any and all of our human understanding)
will stand watch over your hearts and minds
in Jesus...* Philippians 4:7 (The Voice)

Tomorrow I have surgery. Today I opened the blue folder... the one that's been sitting on my dresser, waiting.

For weeks I've known I would open it. I mean... it's not like I can simply NOT open the blue folder. It's from my surgeon... and she said I HAD to.

But ever since my breast cancer diagnosis my life has been in a whirlwind... from a pre-planned anniversary trip to the East Coast to a week-long ministry marathon at a family camp... the timing just hasn't been right to open the blue folder.

That is until now.

So... with my morning coffee in hand, I made my way to the back deck, nestled into a multi-coloured cushion and... *stared* at the blue folder.

It's not that big of a deal, I know. People have cancer surgery every day. But it felt like as soon as I begin to read those pages and acquaint myself (in vivid clarity) with the exact procedures my surgeon will perform... well, that's when it will all become real.

It *is* real.

And so, I opened the blue folder...

Immediately I was met with pages upon pages of "preparation" and "procedure" and "patient recovery" (they do tell you everything!).

Needing to warm up my coffee (twice), the morning slipped away while I was knee-deep in the narrative. But it was while I was in the middle of all of the medical-people jargon that something strange happened.

I began to notice a song playing in the background of my thoughts.

I wasn't thinking about a song. God knows how much I was trying to concentrate on the material I was reading. But there it was. Like a serene soundtrack to a touching movie, the song played on.

It was a soothing song. A calming song. A peaceful song.

It was a song that we don't sing in church anymore... and that's a shame. Because I can't help but wonder how many other people, like me, would find comfort in its message.

"Peace, peace, wonderful peace, coming down from the Father above; sweep over my spirit forever I pray, in fathomless billows of love."

Closing my eyes, I soaked in the words. Taking a deep breath, I just *breathed in* His peace.

> *Closing my eyes, I soaked in the words. Taking a deep breath, I just breathed in His peace.*

And the pages and the instructions and the plans... simply faded into the background.

And the daunting blue folder... became... only paper.

Yes, tomorrow the surgeon will do what she must do. And that's as it should be. But today... today I will do what I must do.

Today I have chosen to be blanketed... in HIS peace.

And in His peace... I am content.

Sips to Savour

♡ Is there a "blue folder" in my life that I
have been avoiding, because opening it would
be a source of stress and fear?

♡ How can I face reality with confidence and
courage today...and be at peace?

Prayer Starter

*Lord God, as I bring my anxious thoughts to You in
prayer, I know I can face my fears with faith. I take
a deep breath in Your presence
and receive Your peace.*

Notes

_____

_____

_____

_____

_____

Good Morning?

And because of His glory and excellence, He
has given us great and precious promises.
2 Peter 1:4 (NLT)

"**G**ood morning."
So many times we say those words without even thinking about them.

Yet often on this unexpected journey, quaint phrases like "good morning" seem out of place... like a betrayal to the very integrity of our current circumstance.

How can anything be *good* when the world you're living in feels *bad*... like it's being dismantled before your very eyes? You keep hoping that if you could only grab it with both hands, you might somehow regain control. And then you realize that's just not going to happen.

Where's the *good* in that?

Perhaps the *good* begins as we remind ourselves that all we can really do, at this moment in time, is pray for calm... and breathe in God's peace.

> *Just as Jesus calmed the sea with His command for "Peace!", we need to allow Him to calm the turbulence in our souls with the same vivid call.*

Just as Jesus calmed the sea with His command for "Peace!", we need to allow Him to calm the turbulence in our souls with the same vivid call.

And we need to remember to breathe.

Deep, calm, slow breaths. Lung expanding... head clearing... vision sharpening breaths.

With every fibre of our being, we need to feel the calm that kind of breathing invites.

And while we're at it, let's draw in the words of the Apostle Paul as expressed in the Amplified Bible...

"...for we walk by faith, not by sight [living our lives in a manner consistent with our confident belief in God's promises]..."
2 Corinthians 5:7 (AMP)

Maybe you need to read the last part of that verse again. Maybe I do too.

"living our lives in a manner consistent with our confident belief in God's promises..."

What are some of God's promises?

He will never leave us (Hebrews 13:5)...

When we go through difficult times He is with us (Isaiah 43:2)...

There is nowhere we can go apart from His love (Romans 8:38)...

As we focus on Him, He gives perfect peace (Isaiah 26:3)...

The peace He gives is divine... and incomprehensible (John 14:27 & Phil 4:7)...

Resting in Him produces quiet confidence (Isaiah 30:15)

He will go before us and make the rough places smooth (Isaiah 45:2)...

In our darkest times, He gives us treasures (Isaiah 45:3)...

He sees our broken heart and stays close, rescuing our crushed spirit (Psalm 34:18)...

He has saved us, washed us, renewed us, by His Holy Spirit (Titus 3:5).

We need to live our lives with a *confident hope* in those promises (and so many more). Yes, things are hard right now. And yes, on the surface it's hard to see the *good*.

But our confidence does not dwell on the surface.

God's Word is our Rock. His faithfulness is our Anchor. And nothing that happens in the shifting sand of our world will ever change that.

And so... in light of all of God's unshakeable promises, there's only one thing left to be said...

I guess it really is a *good* morning.

Sips to Savour

♡ Do I honestly feel that "good morning" is a greeting I can receive with a positive attitude today?

♡ What promises from God's Word do I need to cling to right now as a step of faith that transcends my current circumstance?

Prayer Starter

Dear Lord, I thank You for Your rock-solid Truth and promises that I can stand upon when my life seems to be filled with shifting sand. Today I pause to breathe deeply and receive Your perfect peace.

Notes

_____

_____

_____

_____

_____

_____

_____

_____

_____

_____

Straight from the Source

*I pray that God, the Source of hope, will fill
you completely with joy and peace because
you trust in Him. Then you will overflow
with confident hope through the power of the
Holy Spirit.* Romans 15:13 (NLT)

I love those words of encouragement from the
Apostle Paul. And boy, do I need them!

...fill you completely with joy and peace.

As I consider my life right now, during this very
present difficult season, *somber and turbulent* might
better describe my spirit.

A diagnosis of breast cancer was the first blow, the
first joy-stealer. And then, as if that wasn't enough,
my peace was violently shaken with the pronounce-
ment of needed chemotherapy.

... because you trust in Him.

I trust in Him.

I first gave Jesus my life... my trust... when I was 9 years old. It was a clarion day in my childhood... a mature, clear-thinking, deliberate decision made right in the middle of the care-free life of a little girl. It was real. It was transforming. And on that day, I knew I would never be the same.

That sesame-seed-sized trust was first tested 4 years later when my baby brother died. Only 3 days after he took his first breath... he took his last. And my teenaged heart was broken. Was I angry at God? Yes. Did I question His reasoning? Absolutely. Was my trust in Him still intact? Surprisingly, it was.

And while I still can't explain it, I found that same trust to be still strong years later, at the death of my father, and a decade after that at the passing of my mother.

So, I guess *trusting in God* has never really been my struggle. The source of that trust lies deep within me... an intimate relationship that anchors my soul to the very heart of my loving God.

So that begs the question... why do I still struggle with joy and peace? I mean, if the Scripture is true (which I have no doubt that it is), then...

God, the Source of hope, will fill me completely with

joy and peace because I trust in Him.

Isn't that the way it's supposed to go? So where is the disconnect?

I know it may sound trivial... silly even... but part of me wonders if those words are in the wrong order. Maybe the Apostle Paul, when he was writing them, should've used "command c" to copy and "command v" to paste and simply rearranged the phrases so that the effect *follows* the cause.

> *It all comes back to that foundational, intimate relationship. The giving heart of my loving God.*

Maybe something like this...

Because I trust in Him, God, the Source of hope, will fill me completely with joy and peace.

Like drawing a picture by connecting numbered dots, my spirit needs to be reminded that my trusting heart is already plugged into all the hope and joy and peace it can handle... because the divine Source of it all is so very near.

It all comes back to that foundational, intimate relationship. The giving heart of my loving God. As I anchor my trust in Him, He offers these gifts to me. My wounded heart simply needs to receive them.

Simple. And yet, not.

I once heard it said that *fear causes us to focus on what we see... rather than Who we know.*

For over four decades I've *known* God. For even longer, He's *known* me. And that deep, abiding heart relationship is a direct lifeline to the very Source of hope... and joy... and peace.

And so, on this somber and turbulent day, I have a choice to make.

I choose to hold onto my Anchor, and allow His joy to be my peace.

And if I have to, I will make that choice over and over again.

Because my Anchor's not going anywhere.

And I trust Him.

Sips to Savour

♡ What are the biggest stealers of my joy and peace right now?

♡ Are there any trust issues I have with God from past experiences that may be clogging the flow of joy and peace from the Source?

Prayer Starter

Father God, You are the Source of all hope. Today, from the deepest part of me, I choose to trust You and allow You to fill me completely with Your over-flowing joy and peace.

Notes

Day 13

From "C" to See

... always think about what is true. Think about what is noble, right and pure. Think about what is lovely and worthy of respect. If anything is excellent or worthy of praise, think about those kinds of things. Philippians 4:8 (NIRV)

Cheerful... Chuckle... Calm... Content. Oh, and of course, Coffee. I love all of those words. They're happy words. And they all start with the letter "c."

There are a couple of other words that start with the letter "c" that I'm not that crazy about. They're definitely *not* happy words. One of them, I've seen up-close and personal.

Cancer.

It's a dreaded disease that can strike indiscriminately... from stealing the glow from the rosy-cheeked young... to tarnishing the gleam from the golden years of the old... to everyone in between.

Which is where I find myself.

Since my diagnosis in June, cancer has joined my vocabulary in a very personal way. And I'm still processing the weight of it.

The other word that begins with a "c" is one I've only heard about in muffled voices behind cupped hands. It's a dreaded word. It's a controversial word. It's a word that, when ultimately attached to my diagnosis, caused me to double over in shock. Literally.

Chemotherapy.

Because of certain factors discovered after surgery, my doctor has deemed this treatment as necessary. And I'm still reeling.

Its name might as well be "Goliath" because that's how it makes me feel... like a tiny David standing against a Mt. Everest-sized foe. Small. Insignificant. Vulnerable.

But perhaps it's time to remind myself of how that story ended.

Because when confronting his colossal foe, miniscule David wasn't standing alone. No. He had all of Heaven's armies standing behind him. And even greater still, he had the Commander of those armies, Almighty God Himself, literally towering over everything. And I love how this wee warrior spoke out his faith...

"You come to me with sword, spear, and javelin, but I come to you in the name of the Lord of Heaven's Armies... Today the Lord will conquer you..."
1 Samuel 17:45-46 (NLT)

Oh, how I love his faith! How *I need his faith.*

Confidence.
Courage.
Certainty.
Conviction.

Because although chemotherapy doesn't come at me with sword, spear or javelin, it does come with some pretty potent weapons of its own... fear, uncertainty, nausea, hair loss, and the list goes on.

And while it's important to remember that my "Goliath" isn't any more threatening than David's Goliath... it's more important to remember that David's God (who is also MY God) isn't any less powerful than He was then.

And so, Chemo, I have a message for you...

"You come to me with fear, uncertainty, nausea, hair loss, but I come to you in the name of the Lord of Heaven's Armies... Today the Lord will conquer you..."

Boy, that felt good!

And here are some more "c" words to hang your hat on...

Confidence. Courage. Certainty. Conviction.

All words that come directly from the heart of God... my clear and calming Comforter.

And my favourite...

Christ.

Because HE is the strong and compassionate One.

And He will get me through it all.

Sips to Savour

♡ What intimidating "Goliath" issue is currently staring me down, making me feel tiny and vulnerable?

♡ How does it change my levels of confidence and courage when I realize that my loving, Almighty God is on my side?

Prayer Starter

Father God, thank You for standing with me... before me, beside me, behind me... as I go into battle. Your great love gives me such courage and hope in the face of all my enemies!

Notes

_____

_____

_____

_____

_____

_____

_____

_____

_____

_____

Peace in the Upside Down

*It is I, the Eternal One your God... Who whispers in
your ear, "Don't be afraid. I will help you."*
Isaiah 41:13 (The Voice)

There's something comforting about listening to
the washing machine run. As I sit with my early-morning coffee, I revel in the sound. It tells me
that my household is running smoothly... my family
is being cared for... all is right with the world. It
speaks peace.

I know that's a lot to ask from a nuts and bolts machine. And given my present circumstance it might
even sound funny for me to say it.

You see, this morning I woke up with my world
looking very different. At least the part of my world
that I see in the mirror. Today I woke up for the first
time with no hair.

Since beginning chemotherapy two weeks ago, my hair gradually began falling out, more recently, by the handful. So yesterday, at my request, my long-time hairdresser and dear friend, Elie, came to my home and shaved my head. I sat with my eyes closed, held my husband's hand, and cried through most of it. Elie did too.

> *If we listen closely, we are not alone.*

I know it's only hair... and that it will grow back. I know that I can wear a cap or a scarf or a wig (all of which I plan to try). I know all of these things. But this new corner I've turned now puts an outward face on all of the inward turmoil my body is going through. It lets complete strangers know of my very personal struggle. It lets the whole world know I was diagnosed with cancer. That, for a while, my world is turned upside-down.

Sometimes life is like that. We carry around a hidden heartache, hoping no one else will find out. We think that if we can covertly power through one more day, the world might finally right itself.

But then we realize a startling fact. That, for now, upside-down is our new normal. And that, more importantly, if we listen closely... we are not alone.

And so I go back to the washing machine.

The soothing, reassuring sound of my world running

right-side up. Of my family being cared for. Of my home sounding like a home.

And as I sit and listen, I sense God's oh-so-sweet presence. His voice is my calming anchor and He soothes my weary heart as He says...

"Like the clothes in that nuts and bolts machine, just soak in My peace... sway to the rhythm of my grace... and let me gently wash away the anxiety and distress.

We're in this together.

I'm not going anywhere.

I've got you."

... and I breathe in peace.

Sips to Savour

♡ What seems "upside down" in my life right now, causing me to feel disoriented?

♡ How can I accept what seems to be my "new normal" and receive God's soothing peace on this journey?

~Prayer Starter~

Lord God, I thank You that You are with me now, whispering in my ear, "Don't be afraid." Your calming presence brings me true comfort and fills me with hope.

Notes

_____

_____

_____

_____

_____

_____

_____

_____

_____

_____

_____

Always Holding Me

Praise the Lord; praise God our Saviour!
For each day He carries us in His arms.
Psalm 68:19 (NLT)

Morning... afternoon... evening. No matter what time of day or what we're facing, God is always with us.

Yesterday *morning* I woke up to face treatment #6 of Chemo... and God was with me.

Throughout the *day* I knew He was holding me in His arms.

And as *evening* descended, I slept soundly, knowing He was watching over me.

My faith in God is unshakeable. And in that trust, I find security.

So often, when we are on an unexpected journey, those on the outside will look at us and think that our trust appears misplaced. And I'll concede that point. I mean, look at me. The chemo has taken its toll.

> *Morning... afternoon... evening. No matter what time of day or what we're facing, God is always with us.*

I've lost weight. A lot of it (constant nausea and lack of appetite will do that). My energy level is depleted and my social life is limited. My complexion is dull, my taste buds are bland, and my concentration level is waning... on a good day. And don't forget about my hair... which would be easy to do since it left me weeks ago. ☺

Yes, the reasonable thing to do would be to question the basis for my trust.

They might argue... *Where is the proof that the One you're trusting in is actually listening? Or capable? Or even concerned?*

Well, here's my question for them...

Who said that faith in God required proof?

Doesn't that kind of heart connection live outside of our natural "show me what you can do" world?

The Spirit-inspired writer of Hebrews thought so...

"Faith is the assurance of things you have hoped for, the absolute conviction that there are realities you've never seen."
Hebrews 11:1 (The Voice)

The *assurance*... the absolute *conviction* of unseen realities.

I love that.

Because it is that *assurance* my heart clings to during random sleepless nights. It is that *conviction* my trust is anchored in when facing another uncertain day.

Faith in my unseen God. Because I *know* Him.

And because I *know* Him, I *trust* Him.

No matter what is going on around me (or physically, within me), I have no doubt that HE is beside me, holding me through it all.

And that is a reality that no amount of nausea or hair loss or even skepticism can alter.

Often, on this unexpected journey, acknowledging that deep trust is exactly what we need to do. Because until He clearly reveals the next step, our trust in Him is the only solid ground beneath our feet.

And as we stand there, we can rest in one simple truth.

He who is Trustworthy... will never leave us.

Sips to Savour

♡ Have there been difficult times in my life when I have deliberately chosen to trust God, even though to others that trust seemed misplaced?

♡ What truths do I intimately KNOW about the Lord that help form the solid foundation upon which I'm standing right now?

Prayer Starter

Dear Lord, You have been so faithfully present in the past, and I know You continue to be with me today, despite what other voices might say. Right now, I relax in the security of Your loving arms, and I trust You.

Notes

His Presence Always

I am with you always [remaining with you perpetually—regardless of circumstance, and on every occasion], even to the end of the age. Matthew 28:20 (AMP)

"It's beginning to look a lot like Christmas!" and the celebrations have begun...

Our once drab homes are sparkling with gemstone colours. Our oven-warmed kitchens smell like gingerbread and shortbread. And our buttoned-up wardrobe is now wrapped up in cardigans and candy canes.

Gifts are being purchased... and wrapped... and hidden away for early-morning fun.

And the music. Ah, the music.

It seems everywhere we go the soundtrack of "Joy" and "Noel" and "Silent Night" accompanies us throughout the day.

All great truths. All about Jesus.

Yes, right now, at this precise moment on the calendar, the world at large is aware of the birth of Christ. God-with-us. Emanuel.

The question is... what do they do with it?

And just as important... what do they do with HIM the rest of the year?

What about you and me?

Really, in a lot of ways, we're all very similar.

It's easy to go about our day without really being aware of the presence of God.

It's not that we're ignoring Him. It's just that our lives are so busy that unless we have a reminder, He's simply not in our thoughts.

But oh, those reminders.

They come in various shapes and sizes.

Overwhelming financial stress. The heartache of a broken relationship. An out-of-the-blue doctor's report.

All reminders to us that, even in the busyness of our everyday lives, we need God.

We NEED to be aware of Him.

It's been said that, "Awareness of God is the fruit of the stillness of God."

Taking time for Him... not only when we hear the carols playing... but especially when the music stops.

Hmm. *...the stillness of God.*

Being still with Him. All year long.

Taking time for Him... not only when we hear the carols playing... but especially when the music stops. And the daily grind starts. All over again.

For even when we eventually take down the tree and put away the Christmas sweaters... the Baby from the nativity remains.

May we longingly desire with the Apostle Paul, "... *that I may know Him [experientially, becoming more thoroughly acquainted with Him, understanding the remarkable wonders of His Person more completely]...*" Philippians 3:10 (AMP)

Because what was started in the manger... and

completed on the Cross... and proven by the empty tomb... is only the beginning of our reason to celebrate.

God-with-us.

God forgiving us.

God embracing us.

God IN us.

These are the Christmas gifts we receive all year long.

Sips to Savour

♡ Have I taken the time today to pause and acknowledge the presence of God in my life... even while I'm managing the mundane?

♡ What daily disciplines can I employ to keep the awareness of God's presence at the forefront of my distracted mind?

Prayer Starter

Thank You, Lord, that You are Emmanuel, God-with-us, every day of the year. May I be ever mindful of Your sweet presence in times of both dedicated devotion and day-to-day duty.

Notes

A Shelter in the Storm

The Lord is my rock, my fortress...
Psalm 18:2 (NIV)

Sometimes the weight of this unexpected journey can leave you feeling vulnerable and exposed. You hear the wind picking up and see the sky growing dark, and before you know it, you're running for cover.

And as wonderful as your support system is (whether personal or medical), they can't truly understand the storm that is brewing in your soul, for their horizon doesn't share the same clouds.

This storm goes by many names... *Fear... Uncertainty... Isolation... Pain... Worry.*

And with every windy breath, it taunts you, overwhelming your senses with the smell of an impending downpour.

That's when clarity steps in to remind you of an unflappable Truth. The storm can't touch you, for your faith in God has depleted its power.

But still your heart aches with need...

... to *feel* sheltered.

... to *know* safety.

> *He is everything we need Him to be.*

And that's when we need to remember something else. We need to remember the depth and breadth of Him in Whom our faith is placed.

He is *Almighty* God, yes. But He is also *Faithful* God... *Caring* God... *Active* God... *Intimate* God... *Protective* God... *Conquering* God... and *so much more.*

He is everything we need Him to be.

And often on my unexpected journey, I've needed Him to be my Everything.

And you know what? That's exactly what He wants to be.

In this watchful season, allow Him to be your Everything.

Your mighty Shelter is waiting. In His strong and mighty arms, you can *know* true safety.

Meditate on these promises...

"You are my hiding place from every storm of life... You will protect me from trouble and surround me with songs of deliverance."
Psalm 32:7 (TLB, NIV)

"I love You, Lord;
   You are my strength.
The Lord is my rock, my fortress, and my Saviour;
   my God is my rock, in whom I find protection.
He is my shield, the power that saves me,
   and my place of safety."
Psalm 18:1-2 (NLT)

"God is our shelter and our strength.
   When troubles seem near, God is nearer, and He's ready to help."
Psalm 46:1 (The Voice)

"The Lord Himself will fight for you. Just stay calm."
Exodus 14:14 (NLT)

Sips to Savour

♡ What daunting, dark clouds are looming on my horizon today, causing my anxious heart to pound with fear?

♡ How do I take refuge right now in that secure place of safety God promises to me as His beloved child?

Prayer Starter

God, You are my Rock, my Fortress, my Saviour. When the enemies of my peace try to storm toward me, You are my ever-present Shelter.

Notes

_____

_____

_____

_____

_____

_____

Rest: A Prescription and a Promise

For Jesus is not some high priest who has no sympathy for our weaknesses and flaws. He has already been tested in every way that we are tested; but He emerged victorious...
Hebrews 4:15 (The Voice)

I love how personal Jesus is. He knows exactly what we're going through because He's already been through it.

Rejected. Discouraged. Exhausted. He experienced it all.

Round seven of chemo is behind me and one of its greatest side effects is once again upon me.

Extreme fatigue.

Yet as I look around me, I find so much I need to do. So much *I want to do.*

Take care of my family. Take care of my home. Actively pursue God's call on my life.

All good things, if only my weary body would cooperate.

> *No matter what you and I are facing in life, it's crucial that we set aside time for our bodies... and souls... to rest.*

And while the doctor encourages me to move around as much as I can, he also reiterated the importance of listening to my body. It knows when I simply need to rest.

No matter what you and I are facing in life, it's crucial that we set aside time for our bodies... and souls... to rest.

The Bible is filled with God's promises to provide rest when we seek Him. He actually created us to need Him.

How intimate He is.

Never One to push Himself on us, Almighty God went to great lengths to let us know He is available... waiting... longing to give us what we need.

Rest. In a secure and loving place.

Rest in Him.

The invitation is clear...

"Come with Me by yourselves to a quiet place and get some rest." Mark 6:31 (NIV)

"Learn from Me, for I am gentle and humble of heart. When you are yoked to Me, your weary souls will find rest." Matthew 11:29 (The Voice)

"I have told you these things so that in Me you may have peace..." John 16:33 (NIV)

"My presence will go with you, and I will give you rest." Exodus 33:14 (NLT)

Sips to Savour

♡ Is physical or emotional exhaustion a regular part of my life? If so, how am I getting the rest that I need?

♡ When was the last time I claimed (and acted upon) God's promises to give me rest... for both my body and my soul?

Prayer Starter

Heavenly Father, I thank You for Your many promises to provide rest when I am weary. Please grant me the wisdom and determination to listen to You and to my body, so that I may slow down, recharge, and renew my physical and spiritual strength.

Notes

_____

_____

_____

_____

_____

_____

_____

_____

_____

_____

Treasures in Darkness

*He reveals deep truths and hidden
secrets; He knows what lies veiled in the
darkness; pure light radiates from
within Him.* Daniel 2:22 (The Voice)

I still haven't seen our Christmas lights. My husband put them on the house over a week ago, tweaking, adjusting, and replacing ruined bulbs over the course of several days. He finally has them just the way he wants them. And he wants me to see them.

But I still haven't seen them.

It's not that I don't want to see them. It's just that the best time to get the full impact of his handywork is at night... in the cold... standing at the end of the icy driveway. Brrrrr. (on this current journey, I have only stepped foot outside our door for medical appointments)

But I *will* see the lights. I'm determined to bundle up and make the trek. Because I know that it's in the darkness that light is the most beautiful. And captivating. And awe-inspiring.

> *Not only is He with you during those dark times, He has promised to give you treasures.*

Maybe you're going through the darkness right now. You'd love for someone to turn on the lights because all you see is disappointment. And hopelessness. And you feel so alone.

It's a place of fearful uncertainty, where you can't seem to see your hand in front of your face. You feel blind to the next step. You're in the darkness.

But you need to know something very important. Even in the darkness, you're not alone.

Especially there.

Did you know that God has made a promise to you for when you're in a dark time?

It's true. He says to you...

"I will give you treasures hidden in the darkness—
  secret riches... so you may know that I am
the Lord... the One who calls you by name."
Isaiah 45:3 (NLT)

Not only is He with you during those dark times, He has promised to give you treasures there. Glowing, sparkling, beautiful treasures. Riches that you can only receive by GOING THROUGH THE DARK-NESS.

Wow.

Did you get that?

Some gifts from God we can only receive when we go through dark times.

It's not that He causes the darkness. It's just that He has so many blessings for us when we're there.

And these treasures look different for all of us.

But one thing they all have in common is... they shine. And if we let them, they will light up the dark-ness for those around us who also find themselves in the dark.

And just maybe... through our lives... He will give them hope too.

Because, as we know, it's in the darkness that light

is the most beautiful. And captivating. And awe-inspiring.

Sips to Savour

♡ What darkness is enveloping me, in which I seem to be anxiously stumbling around looking for light?

♡ Have I discovered a "treasure" in my current darkness that spotlights the truth that God is with me and working out His plan for my ultimate good?

Prayer Starter

Thank You Lord for the peace You give as I hold tightly to Your loving hand while walking through the dark unknown. May I find the treasures of blessing You have for me during this time, giving light and hope for my future.

Notes

Rescue, Shelter, Healing

*The Lord is my rock, my fortress, and the
One who rescues me...*
Psalm 18:2 (AMP)

*You are my hiding place from
every storm of life...*
Psalm 32:7 (Living Bible)

*He heals the broken-hearted
and bandages their wounds.*
Psalm 147:2 (NLT)

Sometimes you just need a hiding place. You know what I mean. A safe place where you know that nothing on earth can hurt you.

Oh, it's not a geographical, physical location. But it's real nonetheless.

It's a safe place for your soul.

And sometimes you just need it.

Tomorrow is my 7th round of chemo. And I definitely need that place.

For He's not only our Hiding Place... our Rock... our Fortress. He's also the One who safely delivers us to that sheltered place.

For while my body is in a battle, fighting to rid itself of unwanted disease, my soul is at peace, resting in the shelter of my Warrior King.

You see, I'm not in this battle alone. You're not in your battle alone.

For He's not only our Hiding Place... our Rock... our Fortress. He's also the One who safely delivers us to that sheltered place.

He's the One who rescues us.

From fear. From pain. From uncertainty.

And He does it oh so tenderly... because He knows the toll the battle has already taken.

And He does something else.

His touch not only brings deliverance... it also brings healing.

Mighty in power, He is also the gentle Physician, tenderly touching our bruised hearts... and with the pressure, bringing healing instead of pain.

Rescue. Shelter. Healing.

As we walk through the uncertainty of whatever lies ahead, those three things ARE certain.

They are just as sure as the faithfulness of the One who provides them.

Sips to Savour

♡ From what do I need rescue, shelter or healing?

♡ How can I reach out and receive from the Lord today all that His faithful, loving hands are making available to me?

Prayer Starter

Faithful Heavenly Father, because I am Your precious child, You are ready, willing and more than able to provide for my every need. I come to You in simple faith today to receive all the blessings You long to pour out on me.

Notes

_____

_____

_____

_____

_____

_____

_____

_____

_____

_____

_____

_____

_____

_____

_____

_____

_____

_____

_____

_____

_____

_____

The War for Peace

Those who love Your law have an abundance
of peace, and nothing along their paths can
cause them to stumble.
Psalm 119:165 (The Voice)

A s I traverse my unexpected journey through
cancer, there have been many (thoughtful and
persistent) voices telling me what I should do.

Avoid sugar... and caffeine... and red meat... and
dairy. Don't over-do activity, but don't be too se-
date. Stay away from people, but enjoy uplifting
family time.

And whatever you do, don't be afraid.

Up until that last one, the list was quite do-able.
While staying away from people AND enjoying family bonding could prove tricky, it was something I was
willing to try. But that last one? It's easier said than
done.

Don't be afraid.

I mean, isn't it only natural to be afraid when faced with the unknown? When there seems to be so many questions and very few answers... isn't that a good time to start pacing the floors and biting my fingernails?

> *Headline news is replaced with Heaven's news... and our outlook begins to shift.*

It's worth remembering that the collective voice of those closest to us isn't the only one telling us to calm our fears.

Multiple times throughout His Word, Jesus clearly encourages, *"Do not be afraid."*

And we hear Him. And, as our hearts beat a little faster, we whisper back, *"But why shouldn't I?"*

That's when, with a gentle smile and infinite compassion, God-the-Son lovingly replies, *"I'm so glad you asked."*

With more patience than our fickle faith deserves, He continues,

If you will only trust Me, I will give you...

...a peace that guards your hearts and minds.
(Philippians 4:6-7)

...a peace that is perfect and constant.
(Isaiah 26:3)

...a peace that shadows you and shelters you.
(Psalm 91:1)

...a peace that calms your heart's turbulent storm.
(Mark 4:39)

...a peace that strengthens you and fortifies you.
(Psalm 18:2)

...a peace that soothes your weary soul.
(Matthew 11:28)

...a peace that embraces your wounded heart.
(John 8:11)

...a peace that rescues your crushed spirit.
(Psalm 34:18)

...a peace that the world can't comprehend.
(John 14:27)

And our hearts are once again drawn to His Word.

That's where Almighty God reveals to us His faithfulness, His righteousness, His sovereignty, His wisdom, His holiness. He shows us Himself in a deeper, more intimate way.

That's where we learn of the Father's incredible love

and amazing grace. We see the Son's supreme Sacrifice in the shape of a Cross. We sense the Spirit's divine intervention in the form of a dove, the leap of a flame, the fragrance of an oil, the sweetness of a fruit.

And He becomes real to us.

And as we truly get to know Him in His fulness, our fears no longer appear overwhelming.

Headline news is replaced with Heaven's news... and our outlook begins to shift.

Through reading His Word, we begin to know Him more, and our mountain of worries, cares, and anxieties soon becomes eclipsed by the bright Light of His Son.

And we rest in His warmth.

Only then are we truly able to do what Jesus proclaimed. Only then are we finally able to put the *not* before our *fear*.

We learn to trust.

And we discover a Truth that even a deluge of uncertainty can't overwhelm.

God's perfect peace is more than an emotion. It's a fortress. And fear will never have the ability to breach its walls.

Sips to Savour

♡ Do I find it difficult to live up to the simple yet challenging command, "Do not be afraid?"

♡ Today, how can I draw closer and draw upon the strength of the One and only true Source of my inner peace?

Prayer Starter

As my heart and mind are fixed on You, dear Lord, You will keep me in perfect peace. My fears fade as I draw near to You right now through my praise, prayers and practice of living out Your promises.

Notes

_____

_____

_____

_____

_____

_____

Gifts in the Waiting

But as for me, I will look expectantly for the Lord and with confidence in Him I will keep watch; I will wait [with confident expectation]... My God will hear me.
Micah 7:7 (AMP)

What are you waiting for? What's the next big event in your life that has your attention?

As I'm writing this, Christmas is less than a week away. That's worth waiting for.

Our son and daughter-in-love are awaiting the arrival of their first child (in 2 short weeks!). That's definitely something to keep you on the edge of your seat.

In my life, besides Christmas and the arrival of a new grandson (!), there's something I've been waiting for since the middle of September.

And it happens tomorrow.

Tomorrow I'll have my last chemotherapy treatment.

When I first started chemo back in September, those eight treatments every two weeks felt monumental. They seemed to stretch on forever. It was like the sun was setting on my normal life and my horizon was getting darker by the minute.

So, I braced myself.

And yes, the road was difficult.

So many memories flood my mind with that one word. Difficult. The various side effects of the treatments leading the way. But in the midst of all of the nausea and fatigue and sleepless nights and hair loss and on and on... there was one challenge I hadn't expected.

The waiting.

Waiting for the next infusion.

And it couldn't come soon enough.

Because even though I knew that the poison injected into my body was what was causing my difficulties, I was very aware of one other important fact. This poison was killing any stray cancer cells as well.

And that was the bottom line.

And so... I wait.

Sometimes waiting for something can be a mixed bag. Your joyful anticipation of the end result is intermingled with dread of the process to get there. Like an athlete pushing through the pain, we keep our eyes on the prize, even as our vision is dimmed by sweat and tears and a million questions as to why we're even there.

Sometimes waiting for something can be a mixed bag. Your joyful anticipation of the end result is intermingled with dread of the process to get there.

And yet we push on... as we wait.

But we don't wait alone.

If we will let Him, our compassionate God will give us gifts in the waiting...

We will become surprisingly strong and courageous as we wait (Psalm 27:14).

We will have renewed strength in our bodies as our spirits rise up on wings like eagles as we wait (Isaiah 40:31).

And if we allow Him, He will give us rest as we wait (Psalm 4:8).

So many benefits of waiting with God.

Because no matter what we go through... even after we've reached our goal and claimed our prize... His tender Presence remains.

And knowing that truth makes the long, difficult journey so much sweeter.

Sips to Savour

♡ What am I waiting for that seems to be monopolizing my energy and attention?

♡ Am I anxious and impatient while in the waiting room... or do I see this time as an opportunity to allow God to be present and at work in my life?

Prayer Starter

Heavenly Father, may I keep my focus on You as I wait, knowing that You are working in me what's best for what's next. Thank You for Your strength, peace and rest as I spend this precious time with You.

Notes

Delight in the Details

The Lord directs the steps of the godly.
He delights in every detail of their lives.
Psalm 37:23 (NLT)

During the course of our unexpected journeys, it's easy to get tunnel vision. The headlines in our lives are so bold and glaring that their mere presence demands all of our attention.

The letter from the bank. The severing of the relationship. The initial diagnosis.

Like a glitched video, those big announcements play over and over in our heads until our eyes glaze over and our minds go numb.

And we see nothing else.

But on this journey, as in life, there are so many other scenes that deservedly vie for our attention.

While not necessarily adorned as the *grand revelation,* they carry importance, nonetheless.

They are the details of our lives. And they have intrinsic value.

In our "just the facts" society, the details are the colour commentary of our story. Their palette provides the gentle nuances and subtle shades that bring relief to the stark strokes of an often heavy brush.

They add depth. They reveal beauty.

And quite often, these *by-the-way* revelations have a lasting impact.

Such was the case several times in the Bible...

In John 21, the risen Jesus provided for His weary and wondering disciples a bountiful catch, numbering 153 fish... a clever reassurance of His proven claim that "I AM GOD" (the known numerical value attributed to each Hebrew letter of that phrase equals 153).

In Genesis 16, during an especially vulnerable moment, the emotionally beaten and physically rejected Hagar cried in her distress to the only One who cared for her, *"You are the God who sees me"*... a tender revelation that brought her comfort and peace.

In Lamentations 3, in the middle of his emotional lament over the lost city of Jerusalem, a broken and dejected Jeremiah declared of the Lord, *"Yet this I call to mind... Great is Your faithfulness"*... a timely reminder of the One who is forever unconditionally attentive.

In Psalm 139, a reflective King David took comfort in God's attention to the details of his formation as he prayed, *"You made all the delicate, inner parts of my body and knit me together in my mother's womb"*... a revealing observation of an intimate, steady-handed Creator.

As we travel this unexpected journey, we need to be mindful to never gloss over the hidden blessings in our day-to-day lives.

And in 1 Kings 19, a journey-weakened Elijah listened for God's empowering voice first in a mighty wind, and then in a terrible earthquake, and finally in an intense fire... all to no avail. As is so often the case in our lives, God's voice came to him in the gentleness of a whisper... revealing the unseen nearness of our tender and loving God.

The subtle details.

In the middle of a much larger story, these are hidden gems... as Isaiah recorded, *"treasures in the darkness"* (Isaiah 45:3).

And even though they can easily be seen as footnotes... insignificant details that, when viewed in the midst of the broader picture, seem to pale in significance... it is vital that we remember them.

As we travel this unexpected journey, we need to be mindful to never gloss over the hidden blessings in our day-to-day lives.

An unexpected note on an especially lonely day...

The gift of potted greenery to cheer up an otherwise gloomy room...

A surprise ring of the doorbell delivering a thoughtfully prepared meal.

The details in life.

Because there will come a time when we will need to remember.

Just like tiny sparks emanating from a larger fire, their remembrance will point us back to the beauty and warmth of the Source. And it is in Him that we will once again find comfort in the midst of this often long, dark night of the soul.

As we allow ourselves to focus on the blessing of the details, the God of those details becomes our greater focus.

Because, ultimately, He is our story.

And in Him lies our peace.

Sips to Savour

♡ What headline in my life seems to be defining my current journey? Is it demanding my focus in a negative way?

♡ What hidden gems has God written into the fine print as my story continues to unfold?

Prayer Starter

Thank You, Lord, for your loving attention to the details of my life. I have perfect peace in the knowledge of Your sovereign guidance of each small step along my daily journey.

Notes

_____
_____
_____
_____
_____
_____
_____
_____
_____
_____
_____
_____
_____
_____
_____
_____
_____
_____
_____
_____
_____

Day 24

Navigating with Truth

... If you follow Me, you won't be stumbling through the darkness, because you will have the Light that leads to Life.
John 8:12b (NLT)

This unexpected journey can have so many cares... anxieties... worries.

If we're not careful, it's easy to allow these concerns to overwhelm our senses... for them to overshadow our perception and cloud our judgment.

They can derail our focus.

And before we know it, our fear-driven internal dialogue has slipped into a rut. It's a dangerous pattern of thinking that quickly becomes dark and lonely. It's a rut we would never choose at the outset, but one that, if left unchecked, can take us far from the life-giving Source of our peace.

And to get out of it, we must commit to something. We must deliberately readjust our eyes to HIS Light.

During times in my life when I've felt overwhelmed with so many unanswered questions, I've found such peace when I've chosen to focus instead on what I DO know.

It's like a certain harbour in Italy that can only be reached by sailing up a narrow channel between dangerous rocks and sandbanks. Over the years, many ships had been wrecked in the confining waterway, and so navigation is extremely hazardous.

In order to guide the ships past the dangers and safely into port, a series of lights were mounted on huge poles in the harbour, to clearly identify the route. The captain of the ship knows that when the lights are perfectly lined up in his vision and seen as only one light, the ship can safely proceed through the narrow channel.

Such is the passage through our darkness. Such is the navigation of this unexpected journey.

Yes, we may still have questions. And yes, for many

of them, there is no answer in sight.

During times in my life when I've felt overwhelmed with so many unanswered questions, I've found such comfort when I've chosen to focus instead on what I *DO* know...

God is good. (Psalm 145:9)

God is compassionate. (Psalm 56:8)

God sees me. (Genesis 16:13)

God rescues me. (Proverbs 34:18)

God is my place of safety. (Psalm 18:2)

God is trustworthy. (Psalm 100:5)

God cares about the smallest details of my life. (Psalm 139:1-4)

God will never leave me. (Matthew 28:20)

God is my peace. (John 14:27)

The Bible is filled with these truths and promises (and so many more).

No matter what you're facing today, no matter where your thoughts begin to drift, if you allow the Light of these truths to come into alignment in your spirit, you will have peace as you navigate your journey.

Trust Him who is your Peace.

He loves you so.

"I have loved you with an everlasting love—
out of faithfulness I have drawn you close."

Jeremiah 31:3 (The Voice)

"... casting all your cares [all your anxieties, all
your worries, and all your concerns, once and for
all] on Him, for He cares about you [with deepest
affection, and watches over you very carefully]."

1 Peter 5:7 (AMP)

Sips to Savour

♡ Has my pattern of thinking been in a rut...
focusing on those nagging, unanswered
questions?

♡ How can I readjust my focus in the light of
God's amazing promises and truths...
the things I DO know?

Prayer Starter

*Today, Lord, I surrender my desire to figure
everything out, and I trust in You... in Your
sovereign plan and purpose for my life. With Your
loving hand firmly clutching mine, I am willing to
walk with You, step by step, down
this unfamiliar pathway.*

Notes

_____

_____

_____

_____

_____

_____

_____

_____

_____

_____

Vulnerable and Victorious

When I needed the Lord, I looked for Him;
I called out to Him, and He heard me
and responded. He came and rescued me
from everything that made me so afraid.
Psalm 34:4 (The Voice)

I love how vulnerable David was when he wrote his Psalms.

Afraid... broken... in need of forgiveness. He was transparent about it all.

And God was there, providing exactly what he needed.

I don't know about you, but I'm so much like David. Full of faith one day, crying out for help the next.

I'm so thankful that our amazing God hasn't changed.

He hears us where we are... and He is there.

Patient. Loving. Faithful.

He is all that and more.

> *No matter what you're facing today there is one thing you need to remember... Almighty God is with you.*

No matter what you're facing today, there is one thing you need to remember... Almighty God is with you.

And not only is the God of the Universe standing with you, His very Being surrounding you... He is doing even more.

He is giving you strength.

His strength.

His stand-up-strong... nothing-can-bring-me-down... together-we-can-do-this strength.

His pressing-through-the-pain...trusting-through-the-uncertainty... confident-beyond-all-doubt-that-God-is-in-control strength.

That strength.

Through every fibre of your being. Every cell. From your head to your feet.

Through all of you.

God is with you. And HE is your strength. Call out to Him. He will rescue you.

You are NOT alone.

Fear not, for I am with you; be not dismayed, for I am your God. I will strengthen you, Yes, I will help you, I will uphold you with My righteous right hand. Isaiah 41:10 (NKJV)

Sips to Savour

♡ Am I being honest and vulnerable with God and trusted friends about my feelings and fears?

♡ Knowing that He is indeed with me, how can I tap into God's limitless strength for today's step on my journey?

Prayer Starter

Thank You, Lord Jesus, that You are with me and that I can share my deepest feelings with You. By Your Spirit, You are guiding me, calming me, and healing me. I stand on Your Word that "I can do all things through [You] who strengthens me" (Philippians 4:13).

Notes

Ready or Not

The Eternal is my rock, my fortress... the
stronghold in which I hide...
Psalm 18:2 (The Voice)

Hide and go seek. It was always one of my favourite games as a child. And when our kids were growing up, it was one of their favourites too.

You know the game. It's basically broken down into two parts... You have your "hider" and you have your "seeker." I always liked being the hider.

Usually your hiding spot was someplace dark and closed in... some place no one would ever think of looking. That's the whole point of the game, isn't it? To hide in a place where the seeker would never think to check. It wasn't easy.

Now to be fair, you usually didn't have very long to scout out the perfect spot to hide. According to the rules, it was only until the count of 10... and then the dreaded words would ring out, "Ready or not, here I come!"

Ready or not.

Hmmm...

When you think about it, those are some of the scariest words you could ever hear.

Ready or not... here the unexpected comes!

Ready or not... here heartbreak comes!

Ready or not... here cancer comes!

Ready or not.

We hear those words in life and we panic.

Without even the count of 10 to prepare, we scurry around searching for the best place to hide our vulnerability... to tuck away our pain.

And just like our childhood game, the place we find is usually dark and small and extremely uncomfortable. But we convince ourselves it's safe, and so we dig in deep for the long haul.

But what if it doesn't have to be that way? What if the One who loves us most offers a hiding place that is spacious and lush? What if His idea of safety has more to do with light and strength than it does with darkness and fear?

What if it's a place of companionship, not isolation? A place of intimacy, not loneliness?

The good news is... it is.

And what if He has already told us where it is?

The best news is... He absolutely has.

"He who takes refuge in the shelter of the Most High will be safe in the shadow of the Almighty... His faithfulness will form a shield around you, a rock-solid wall to protect you."
Psalm 91:1, 4 (The Voice)...

"My God is my rock, in whom I find protection. He is my shield... my place of safety."
2 Samuel 22:3 (NLT)...

"The Eternal is my rock, my fortress... the stronghold in which I hide..."
Psalm 18:2 (The Voice)...

"The Eternal keeps [me] safe, so close to Him that His shadow is a cooling shade to [me]."
Psalm 121:5 (The Voice)...

The One who loves us most provides a shelter where we can relax. No nervous waiting. No claustrophobic restrictions. Only safety.

And as we finally settle into that secret place where fear and heartache can't find us, we discover something surprising. The game has lost its power.

We don't need to hide anymore.

Our once-secret hiding place has become our heart's permanent dwelling place, and we don't care who knows.

As the Apostle Paul so exuberantly put it in the book of Romans...

"We find ourselves standing where we always hoped we might stand—out in the wide-open spaces of God's grace and glory, standing tall and shouting our praise."
Romans 5:2 (MSG)

Like a child with arms outstretched in a flowering meadow, we sing and twirl and relish every second. With the sun warming our face and the Son protecting our heart... fear's power has lost its hold.

And we discover something else. Something surprising, and yet infinitely comforting.

We discover that this space is not simply some ethereal place that our heart runs to. It's actually so much more.

Encompassing our mind... our soul... our body...

this place is pure and clean and unaffected by our current circumstance. It is tactile, yet transcendent. It is outside of time, yet has perfect timing. It is free and wide, yet intimate and close.

And we are so much more when we're there.

No longer hiding from a threatening predator, worrying that fear's scent will give us away, we are standing tall, radiating peace and exuding confidence in the One who never leaves us. The One who unequivocally promised that He never would (Hebrews 13:5).

> *The One who loves us most provides a shelter where we can relax. No nervous waiting. No claustrophobic restrictions. Only safety.*

And we realize we now know how to answer the call.

The next time fear wants to play its little game of seeking out this majestic, contented place, we know just what to say.

Ready or not?

No thanks. I'm good.

I'm not going to play this game anymore.

♡ What "ready or not" moment in my life has caused me to fearfully run and hide in a difficult place of my own making?

♡ How can I find a true place of safety in God and victory over fear's constant games?

Prayer Starter

Eternal God, You are my Rock and Fortress in Whom I find ultimate security. Thank You that I can run into Your open, loving arms and find complete peace.

Notes

_____

_____

_____

_____

_____

Fear's Big Secret

*Faith shows the reality of what we hope for;
it is the evidence of things we cannot see.*
Hebrews 11:1 (NLT)

As we do our best to navigate through our unexpected and difficult journey, it's easy to feel
overwhelmed.

Our emotions run high as our fuses run short, and in
the midst of it all, we do our best to keep fear at bay.

We know it's always there, lurking in the shadows
of our quiet moments... taunting with its endless
threats of "what if?"

So, we take a deep breath and face down our fear,
all the while hoping we're strong enough to resist its
cruel little game.

But there's something we need to know.

Fear has a secret.

And it's a big one.

It's a secret that fear would rather keep quiet, one that instantly robs it of its power. It's a secret we would do well to remember.

Fear can't survive in a faith environment.

Now, for some of us, that revelation brings freedom... we feel exhilarated at its simplicity.

Faith kills fear. Our faith in God goes deep. We can do that.

But for others of us, when placed on balancing scales, our fear far outweighs our faith. And this realization only increases our fear.

Talk about a "catch 22!"

Anxiety can be a tricky thing. In this fallen world, we WILL feel anxious. Contagious viruses, both the kinds that affect us physically and those that attack us spiritually, are very much a reality. And as we face them, fear is often our first opponent.

So the question arises, how do we conquer our feared foe?

According to Jesus, the first thing we need to do is throw away the scales. We need to resist the urge to play by fear's rules, for this battle is not rated in equal measures. In Matthew chapter 17 Jesus said...

"... if you had faith even as small as a mustard seed, you could say to this mountain, 'Move from here to there,' and it would move..." Matthew 17:20 (NLT)

Mustard-seed-sized faith can move mountains of fear.

> *Mustard-seed-sized faith can move mountains of fear.*

Did we get that?

I don't know about you but that's the best news I've heard all day.

So often it's easy to see our circumstance as a mighty Goliath, looming large over our David-sized faith. We see its sharpened sword and hear its thundering threats, and we feel small and vulnerable and frightfully exposed.

But thankfully, that is not our reality.

It's been said that "fear causes us to focus on what we see rather than what we know."

And according to Jesus, what we KNOW is this...

The outcome of this battle is NOT dependent on the size of our faith muscles. Because even if they're small, with the infusion of God's power, they are mighty. And they can conquer any foe... especially fear.

So the next time fear threatens you, arrogantly mocking with its mountain of anxiety, take out your faith seed.

And with all of the power and authority of Heaven behind you, tell that mountain to get out of your way.

And be amazed at what even a little bit of faith will do.

Sips to Savour

♡ Do I tend to let the fear of "what if" scenarios outweigh what my faith knows is the Truth?

♡ How can I activate my "mustard seed" faith to take authority over the mountain that's looming on my horizon?

Prayer Starter

Oh God, I know that all things are possible with You. So by faith, I speak to my mountain of fear and command it to Go! I do this by the authority of the Name of my Saviour and Lord, Jesus Christ.

Notes

Heart Monitor

Above all else, guard your heart,
for everything you do flows from it.
Proverbs 4:23 (NIV)

Sometimes when going through a difficult season in life we need to give ourselves a check-up.

So, here goes...

How is your heart?

Before you check your pulse, I should clarify what I'm asking.

How is your heart... the real you...the person you are when no one is around?

Still unsure?

According to one author, "The heart, according to

the Bible, is part of man's spiritual makeup. It is the place where emotions and desires begin; it is that which drives the will of man towards action."

King Solomon was very aware of that when he warned,

"Above all else, guard your heart, for everything you do flows from it." Proverbs 4:23 (NIV)

It's the place where emotions and desires and actions begin. Good or bad, they spring forth from there.

It's no wonder the psalmist David asked God to...

"Search me... and know my heart; test me and know my anxious thoughts." Psalm 139:23

And...

"Create in me a clean heart..." Psalm 51:10

And Jesus highlighted our heart's importance when He proclaimed it a vital part of the greatest commandment...

"Love the Lord your God with all your heart..." Matthew 22:37

Hmmm... the greatest commandment... has to do with our heart.

I don't know about you, but it really makes me want

to take stock of mine.

How is my heart? How drastic are my emotions? How righteous are my desires? How God-honouring are my actions?

They all have a direct reflection on the condition of my heart. Now that puts things into perspective.

And ever so patiently the One who IS faithful whispers... don't worry... I've got you.

And if we were to honestly take measure of our natural inclinations, we'd admit that sometimes our emotions can get the best of us... and our desires are selfish and vain... and our actions are anything but pleasing to God.

And we worry that without emergency surgery, we may not recover.

But that's when it happens.

Just as we're wondering if all is lost ... we hear a Voice. And His words echo in the empty chamber where devotion and commitment should live.

And ever so patiently, the One who IS faithful whispers... don't worry... I've got you...

"I will plant a new heart and new spirit inside of

you. I will take out your stubborn, stony heart and give you a willing, tender heart of flesh."
Ezekiel 36:26 (The Voice)

As we invite Him to, God gives us a willing, tender heart... one focused on HIS desires, with actions reflecting HIS Spirit.

And soon the condition of our heart becomes stable... and dependable.

And as our pulse beats out the steady rhythm of a committed life, we realize something. He didn't just give us a new heart. He gave us HIS heart.

And THAT makes all the difference.

Sips to Savour

♡ Because my emotions and desires spring from my heart, it is imperative that I ask myself this telling question... How is my heart today?

♡ What do I need to do in order for God's Holy Spirit to soften my heart and bring my passions in line with His?

Prayer Starter

*Dear God, I pray as the Psalmist David prayed,
"Search me and know my heart; test me and know
my anxious thoughts"... and also "Create in me a
clean heart." Thank You for Your work
of grace in me.*

Notes

_____

_____

_____

_____

_____

_____

_____

_____

_____

_____

Day 29

Shaken

We will not be afraid, even if the earth is shaken and the mountains fall into the center of the sea... Psalm 46:2 (NLV)

Times of shaking hit us all. A relationship that is broken ... Finances that are evaporated... Health that is compromised. All of it is world-shaking to us.

The diagnosis of breast cancer was an unexpected tremor beneath my feet. And then with each subsequent "update" my world continued to experience aftershocks.

How do you keep standing when your foundation seems to be shifting? How do you keep breathing when the oxygen is being sucked from the room? Where do you go for hope when you're surrounded by voices asking the same questions?

Perhaps this is where you find yourself. I know what

you're going through.

If I could offer any advice, it would be this...

First, be real with what you're feeling, BUT don't allow your feelings to lead the way.

> *Give your feelings a voice... but not the final say.*

Give your feelings a voice... but not the final say.

When I was first diagnosed, my feelings ran the gamut. Shock. Fear. Grief. I had sleepless nights and teary days. It was the way I processed the news. But you need to know one thing... those were my EMOTIONS... my natural reaction to my initial trauma.

But I couldn't let them touch my faith.

Because my faith in God is in ALL that He is... Loving... Compassionate... Intimate... Majestic... All-Knowing... All-Caring... All-Powerful... (and so much more).

THAT is my foundation. The substance of my faith.

And for me, nothing can shake that.

My second loving piece of advice is this...

If you don't have that kind of unshakable faith in

God, ask for it.

Because He longs to give it to you.

In our natural world, questions, fear and panic rule the day. But faith in God transcends the natural. It ushers us into His super-natural. Into that place where fear has no power.

And it all starts with relationship. An intimate relationship that begins with a single step of surrender.

We need to consciously let go of our preconceived notions of how life is supposed to look... and then bravely take the Hand of the Giver of Life itself.

We need to surrender our very life, and every step of this unexpected journey, to God.

His Hand is strong and steady... His grip gentle and secure.

And as He leads us through this foreign land, we find peace in His presence, and our hearts find rest in His warmth.

And in the midnight hour, when fear attempts to do its best work, He draws us close as He holds up His Hand and says, "No, you're not going to touch My child."

And there we find rest.

And as we do, we discover something even more significant.

This new-found relationship isn't only for the dark nights of our soul. No. It is light and fresh and freedom itself... and it is beautifully interwoven into all of the shades of our life's tapestry. And as we willingly open up all that we are to Him, He lavishly pours out all that He is into us.

And He becomes our foundation. And our faith in Him is unshakable.

No matter what terrifying quaking our world may experience, we will not be moved.

Because the One who holds our hand is completely in control.

∽ Sips to Savour ∽

♡ In times of shaking, do I allow my feelings to take the lead in my inner dialogue?

♡ What can I do today to walk in a more intimate relationship with my Saviour, fully surrendered to Him and holding tightly to His strong, loving, guiding Hand?

Prayer Starter

Dear God, though it feels like the ground is shaking beneath my feet, I know that You are my solid foundation. I surrender afresh to Your Lordship over my life, and I walk peacefully forward in Your loving and secure embrace.

Notes

Thankful... For Good Reason

Give thanks to the Lord, for He is good!
His faithful love endures forever.
1 Chronicles 16:34 (NLT)

Sometimes in life we just have to stop and ask ourselves, "What am I thankful for?" To really think about it. Recently, I know I have.

What am I thankful for?

On the surface, ever since my breast cancer diagnosis, the "what am I NOT thankful for" side of the paper has filled up. This terrifying interruption has brought with it heart-stopping fear and teeth-clenching pain. Fever and infections. Nausea and hair loss. ER trips and hospital stays. Definitely not thankful for those.

But it has also ushered in something else... a trust in God that goes deeper and is greater than anything I've ever known. And with it, a deep-rooted assurance that HE is in control.

> *I am so much safer going into the deep with Him... than I ever was wading through the shallows alone.*

But the question remains.

What am I thankful for?

My list might just surprise you. I know it surprised me.

I am thankful for...

Sleepless nights... because it's in the quiet of my room that I sense God's comforting presence.

Lack of appetite... because it helps me realize all of the "filler foods" I was constantly grazing on aren't worth the empty calories they provide.

Constant fatigue... because it's in the "down time" that I finally understand what it means to "rest in the Shadow of the Almighty" (Psalm 91:1).

Hair loss... because, unlike the "beauty culture" around us (of which I was a card-carrying member), I no longer look to the mirror to gauge my value.

What am I thankful for?

I am thankful for this healing journey.

And even though I'm not crazy about all of the twists and turns this journey has taken, Jesus has taken me deeper in His unfathomable love than I ever thought possible.

And this thing I know...

I am so much safer going into the deep with Him... than I ever was wading through the shallows alone.

Sips to Savour

♡ What is something I can be thankful for today that might seem surprising?

♡ Have the challenges of my current journey led me to question or confirm God's sovereign control of my life?

Prayer Starter

Dear Lord, may I learn to be thankful in ALL things, knowing that You are truly in control and working out everything according to Your purpose for me... because I am Your beloved child.

Notes

_____

_____

_____

_____

_____

_____

_____

_____

_____

_____

_____

_____

_____

_____

_____

_____

_____

_____

_____

_____

_____

The Crown

[God] pours out grace on the humble...
Come close to the one true God.
James 4:6, 8 (The Voice)

I've never worn a crown. Never. Not for dress-up as a little girl or even as a Princess for trick-or-treating.

I've had a few friends who have competed in pageants, and they wore crowns. Radiant, glorious, beautiful crowns. An outward symbol of hours and hours of study and practice and accomplishment. A much-deserved adornment for a highly-proficient woman.

I wonder where they keep them, these glittering treasures. On a shelf to display? In a box for safe-keeping?

In Great Britain, the priceless Crown Jewels are kept

in the Tower of London. Seems like a pretty safe place to store your crown.

But as for me... I've never worn one. However, while reading in God's Word I found that HE might disagree.

In the book of 1 Corinthians we're told that...

"A woman's hair is her ornament [crown] and glory." 1 Corinthians 11:15 (AMP)

Another translation says,

It *"radiates her beauty and acts as a natural veil."* (The Voice)

And yet another,

It is her *"pride and joy."* (NLT)

In essence, the message is that our hair can actually be seen as a crown. So no matter who we are, we have been adorned with this "ornament of glory."

As women, our hair can be a funny thing.

For as long as I can remember, I've had a love/hate relationship with mine. I love that it has a good memory (they say fine hair does that), and I hate that it's fine (although my hair dresser says I have a lot of it, whatever that means).

I inherited its blond colour from my Dad and passed it down to one of our three kids.

I've cut it... permed it... high-lighted it... and low-lighted it. I've had it short and long and everything in between.

And for the most part, it's been a pretty enjoyable journey.

Sounds pretty shallow, I know.

But I can't help but think the hair/crown connection just might go deeper than that. For like my friends in pageants, if their crowns symbolize a life devoted to practice and study and accomplishment, our lives' crowns do the same.

They represent a life of determined commitment.

Of steady dedication.

Of unseen sacrifice.

For even if we've never donned an evening gown... our crown has value.

But here's the twist... what do you do when you're battling cancer? A disease that has no respect for pride and joy and glory. One that demands sacrifice. One that takes away your crown.

Two weeks into my three-month chemo treatments,

I lost my hair. All of it.

Coming out in handfuls at first, I finally asked my dear friend and hairdresser to come to my home and shave my head.

To remove my crown.

> *"...and they throw down their crowns before the throne, saying, 'Worthy are You, our Lord and God, to receive the glory and the honor and the power...'"*
> Revelation
> 4:10-11 (AMP)

And he did. Tenderly. Reverently.

And after the sound of the buzzer faded and my many tears dried, I sat holding what was left of my hair.

And I just looked at it.

I couldn't throw it away. I don't know why. I just couldn't. Maybe because it somehow represented my life. So, I simply placed it in a zip-lock bag. And then I quietly put it under my bed.

I know it sounds silly. I mean, what a strange place to store a crown. But you need to know something. My storage place is only temporary.

In the book of Revelation, the Apostle John is given a glimpse of an event that will one day take place in Heaven.

In worshipful awe, there will be a processional of the faithful who...

"... fall down before Him who sits on the throne... and they throw down their crowns before the throne, saying, 'Worthy are You, our Lord and God, to receive the glory and the honor and the power...'"
Revelation 4:10-11 (AMP)

Can't you just picture it? There, at the base of the Throne of the only One who is truly worthy to receive them, lie the crowns. The radiant, glorious, crowns. A mountain of glittering beauty. The sum total of any accomplishments or position accumulated during a life's journey on earth.

It's been said that England's Queen Victoria wished for Jesus' Second Coming during her reign so she could literally remove her crown and lay it at His feet.

I've seen pictures of her crown. What a sight that would be. Adorned in all of her regal glory, the exceedingly revered Queen respectfully submitting herself to the Highest of all Authorities, and with bowed head, presenting Him with her finest.

Wow. What a sight indeed.

And then there's me. With my zip-lock baggie. No sparkle. No jewels. No glory or flourish or spectacle. Just a lowly daughter holding in her hands what's left of her treasured offering. Of her unadorned life.

Not an unblemished life, but one aspiring to unwavering commitment... pursuing steady determination... attempting unseen sacrifice.

Just the life of an ordinary woman being surrendered to an extraordinary God.

What a sight *that* would be (simple as it is).

And you know what? I'm okay with that. For while that little baggie may not mean much to anyone else, my heart tells me it's precious to Him.

It represents my life...my crown. The only one I've ever had.

And even though it will most likely pale in comparison to what has already been given, I will wait with the multitudes as I humbly approach His Throne... the Throne of the One who is my Saviour... my Everything.

And He will see me.

And know me.

And tenderly smile.

And He will watch me as there, right beside Queen Victoria...

... I lovingly lay my crown at His feet.

Sips to Savour

♡ What do I consider as my "crown" in terms of awards and achievements?

♡ In addition to what will happen in Heaven, how can I humbly lay my crown at the feet of Jesus today?

Prayer Starter

Dear Jesus, all that I am and all I have accomplished I lay down before You. As You so amazingly exemplified, help me to foster an attitude of humility in my life, until one day I can present everything to You... face to Face.

Notes

Meaningful Scriptures

To "Percolate" On

"It is the Spirit who gives life...
The words I have spoken
to you are spirit and life."
~ Jesus
John 6:63 (AMP)

Coffee with Him

*T*he following Scriptures represent some of the many Bible verses that have been particularly meaningful to me during my unexpected journey. Some I discovered during my quiet time with God... others were sent to me by caring friends... but all of them are inspired by the Spirit of God Himself to deliver to our hearts peace and security and power and grace (among so many other things).

These Scriptures are divided into two sections. The first collection is encouragement to anyone who is facing a difficult storm in life, no matter what form it takes. The second collection is specifically focused on healing for those whose storm is health related.

I encourage you to percolate on one or two each day, even printing some out and placing them around the house, as I often did. Several of them found a home in my bedroom, on my bathroom mirror, on the fridge door and other places.

As you spend time soaking in God's presence this way, may your heart be blanketed in His powerful, comforting and healing Words.

~ Ann

UPDATE: As of February of 2020, the latest test results have come back from my oncologist. He has officially declared me "cancer free." Praise God!

Coffee with Him

Part One

God's Words of Life
for a Difficult Journey

"He heals the broken-hearted And binds up their wounds [healing their pain and comforting their sorrow]." Psalm 147:3 (AMP)

~

"They overcame... by the blood of the Lamb and by the word of their testimony..."
Revelation 12:11 (NKJV)

~

"Let us hold tightly without wavering to the hope we affirm, for God can be trusted to keep His promise." Hebrews 10:23 (NLT)

"Let us seize and hold tightly the confession of our hope without wavering, for He who promised is reliable and trustworthy and faithful [to His word]." Hebrews 10:23 (AMP)

~

"I know the Lord is always with me. I will not be shaken, for He is right beside me.

No wonder my heart is glad, and I rejoice. My body rests in safety." Psalm 16:8-9 (NLT)

"Let the weakling say 'I am strong.'" Joel 3:10 (NIV)

"Let that vine cling to Me for safety, let it find a good and whole life with Me, let it hold on for a good and whole life." Isaiah 27:5 (MSG)

"Be still, and know that I am God!"
Psalm 46:10 (NLT)

"Be still, be calm, see, and understand I am the True God." Psalm 46:10 (The Voice)

"I pray that God, the Source of hope, will fill you completely with joy and peace because you trust in Him. Then you will overflow with confident hope through the power of the Holy Spirit."
Romans 15:13 (NLT)

"In the morning let me hear about Your faithful love, because I've put my trust in You. Show me the way I should live, because I trust You with my life."
Psalm 143:8 (NIRV)

"Keep your eyes open, hold tight to your convictions, give it all you've got, be resolute, and love without stopping."
1 Corinthians 16:13-14 (MSG)

"...I am with you to deliver you," says the Lord.
Jeremiah 1:8 (NKJV)

"Because [she] clings to Me in love,
I will rescue [her] from harm;
I will set [her] above danger.
Because [she] has known Me by name,
[She] will call on Me, and I will answer.
I'll be with [her] through hard times;
I'll rescue [her] and grant [her] honor.
I'll reward [her] with many good years on this earth and let [her] witness My salvation."
Psalm 91:14-16 (The Voice)

"Praise the Lord; praise God our Saviour!
For each day He carries us in His arms."
Psalm 68:19 (NLT)

"God who began the good work within you will keep
right on helping you grow in His grace until His
task within you is finally finished on that day when
Jesus Christ returns."
Philippians 1:6 (TLB)

"The Lord will work out His plans for my life— for
Your faithful love, O Lord, endures forever."
Psalm 138:8 (NLT)

"We are confident that God is able to orchestrate
everything to work toward something good and
beautiful when we love Him and accept His
invitation to live according to His plan."
Romans 8:28 (The Voice)

"The Lord Himself will fight for you. Just stay
calm." Exodus 14:14 (NLT)

"So do not be afraid. I am with you.
  Do not be terrified. I am your God.
I will make you strong and help you.
  I will hold you safe in My hands.
  I always do what is right."
Isaiah 41:10 (NIRV)

"You don't have to be afraid. I am with you. I am your God. I will make you strong and help you. I will hold you safe in My hands."
Isaiah 41:10 (ERV)

"I will give rest to those who are tired. I will satisfy those who are weak."
Jeremiah 31:25 (NIRV)

"God is within her, she will not fall;
  God will help her at break of day."
Psalm 46:5 (NIV)

"This I declare about the Lord:
He alone is my refuge, my place of safety;
  He is my God, and I trust Him."
Psalm 91:2 (NLT)

"The Lord directs the steps of the godly.
    He delights in every detail of their lives.
Though they stumble, they will never fall,
    for the Lord holds them by the hand."
Psalm 37:23-24 (NLT)

"Keep trusting in the Lord and do what is right in
His eyes. Fix your heart on the promises of God and
you will be secure, feasting on His faithfulness.
Make God the utmost delight and pleasure of your
life, and He will provide for you what you desire the
most." Psalm 37:3-4 (TPT)

"On the day I called, You answered me;
And You made me bold and confident with
[renewed] strength in my life."
Psalm 138:3 (AMP)

"I love you, Lord;
    You are my strength.
The Lord is my rock, my fortress, and my Saviour;
    my God is my rock, in whom I find protection.
He is my shield, the power that saves me,
    and my place of safety."
Psalm 18:1-2 (NLT)

"For I am convinced [and continue to be convinced—beyond any doubt] that neither death, nor life, nor angels, nor principalities, nor things present and threatening, nor things to come, nor powers, nor height, nor depth, nor any other created thing, will be able to separate us from the [unlimited] love of God, which is in Christ Jesus our Lord." Romans 8:1, 38-39 (AMP)

"Jesus said, 'Peace I leave with you; My [perfect] peace I give to you; not as the world gives do I give to you. Do not let your heart be troubled, nor let it be afraid. [Let My perfect peace calm you in every circumstance and give you courage and strength for every challenge.]'" John 14:27 (AMP)

"You are the God who sees me." Genesis 16:13 (NIV)

"Now may the Lord of peace Himself grant you His peace at all times and in every way [that peace and spiritual well-being that comes to those who walk with Him, regardless of life's circumstances]." 2 Thessalonians 3:16 (AMP)

"Therefore, if anyone is in Christ [that is, grafted in, joined to Him by faith in Him as Savior], he is a new creature [reborn and renewed by the Holy Spirit]; the old things [the previous moral and spiritual condition] have passed away. Behold, new things have come [because spiritual awakening brings a new life]." 2 Corinthians 5:17 (AMP)

"Awake, my soul!... I will praise you, Lord... For great is Your love, reaching to the heavens; Your faithfulness reaches to the skies."
Psalm 57:8-11 (NIV)

"You are my hiding place from every storm of life... You will protect me from trouble and surround me with songs of deliverance."
Psalm 32:7 (TLB, NIV)

"I love You, Lord;
    You are my strength.
The Lord is my rock, my fortress, and my Saviour;
    my God is my rock, in whom I find protection.
He is my shield, the power that saves me,
    and my place of safety."
Psalm 18:1-2 (NLT)

*"God is our shelter and our strength.
    When troubles seem near, God is nearer, and He's
ready to help."*
Psalm 46:1 (The Voice)

"Awake, awake... Clothe yourself in strength."
Isaiah 52:1 (NIV)

*"Morning by morning He wakens me
and opens my understanding to His will."*
Isaiah 50:4 (NLT)

*"Praise the Lord; praise God our Saviour!
For each day He carries us in His arms."*
Psalm 68:19 (NLT)

*"God provides for those He loves, even while they
are sleeping."*
Psalm 127:2 (The Voice)

"Now let Your unfailing love comfort me, just as You promised me, Your servant. Surround me with Your tender mercies so I may live, for Your instructions are my delight."
Psalm 119:76-77 (NLT)

"Our weapons are divinely powerful for the destruction of fortresses. We are destroying sophisticated arguments and every exalted and proud thing that sets itself up against the [true] knowledge of God, and we are taking every thought and purpose captive to the obedience of Christ..." 2 Corinthians 10:4-5 (AMP)

"I continually long to know the wonders of Jesus more fully and to experience the overflowing power of His resurrection working in me."
Philippians 3:10 (TPT)

*"I will be your God throughout your lifetime...
 I made you, and I will care for you.
 I will carry you along and save you."*
Isaiah 46:4 (NLT)

"Be strong. Take courage. Don't be intimidated. Don't give [your worries] a second thought because God, your God, is striding ahead of you. He's right there with you. He won't let you down; He won't leave you." Deuteronomy 31:6 (MSG)

"Let all that I am wait quietly before God, for my hope is in Him...
He only is my rock and my salvation;
My fortress and my defense, I will not be shaken or discouraged.
On God my salvation and my glory rest;
He is my rock of [unyielding] strength, my refuge is in God." Psalm 62:5-7 (NLT), (AMP)

"You are my hiding place!
You protect me from trouble,
and You put songs in my heart
because You have saved me."
Psalm 32:7 (CEV)

"You are my hiding place from every storm of life..."
Psalm 32:7 (Living Bible)

"For God has not given us a spirit of fear and timidity, but of power, love, and self-discipline."
2 Timothy 1:7 (NLT)

"... His Spirit fills us with power..."
2 Timothy 1:7 (GNT)

⌒⌒

"The Eternal is my shepherd, He cares for me always. He provides me rest in rich, green fields beside streams of refreshing water. He soothes my fears; He makes me whole again, steering me off worn, hard paths to roads where truth and righteousness echo His name. Even in the unending shadows of death's darkness, I am not overcome by fear. Because You are with me in those dark moments, near with Your protection and guidance, I am comforted. You spread out a table before me, provisions in the midst of attack from my enemies; You care for all my needs, anointing my head with soothing, fragrant oil, filling my cup again and again with Your grace. Certainly Your faithful protection and loving provision will pursue me where I go, always, everywhere. I will always be with the Eternal, in Your house forever."
Psalm 23 (The Voice)

⌒⌒

*"Wait patiently for the Lord.
    Be brave and courageous.
    Yes, wait patiently for the Lord."*
Psalm 27:14 (NLT)

⌒⌒

"In the day when I cried out, You answered me,
And made me bold with strength in my soul."
Psalm 138:3 (NKJV)

$\backsim$

"... you will call, and the Lord will answer;
you will cry for help, and He will say: Here am I."
Isaiah 58:9 (NIV)

$\backsim$

"But those who wait for the Lord [who expect,
look for, and hope in Him] Will gain new
strength and renew their power;
They will lift up their wings [and rise up close to
God] like eagles [rising toward the sun];
They will run and not become weary,
They will walk and not grow tired."
Isaiah 40:31 (AMP)

$\backsim$

"The Lord says, 'I will guide you along the best
pathway for your life. I will advise you and watch
over you.'" Psalm 32:8 (NLT)

$\backsim$

"I stand silently before the Lord, waiting for Him to rescue me. For salvation comes from Him alone. Yes, He alone is my Rock, my Rescuer, Defense and Fortress. Why then should I be tense with fear when troubles come?"
Psalm 62:1-2 (TLB)

"Give praise to the Lord.
   He has heard my cry for His favor.
The Lord gives me strength. He is like a shield that keeps me safe.
   My heart trusts in Him, and He helps me.
My heart jumps for joy.
   With my song I praise Him."
Psalm 28:6-7 (NIRV)

"Let Your unfailing love surround [me], Lord,
   for [my] hope is in You alone."
Psalm 33:22 (NLT)

"May Your constant love be with [me]..."
Psalm 33:22 (GNT)

"...drench [me] with Your endless love..."
Psalm 33:22 (The Voice)

"God has come to rescue me;
    I will trust in Him and not be afraid,
For the Eternal, indeed, the Eternal is my strength
and my song.
    My very own God has rescued me."
Isaiah 12:2 (The Voice)

"Satisfy us each morning with Your unfailing love,
    so we may sing for joy to the end of our lives.
Give us gladness in proportion to our former
misery!
    Replace the evil years with good.
Let us, Your servants, see You work again;
    let our children see Your glory.
And may the Lord our God show us His approval
    and make our efforts successful.
    Yes, make our efforts successful!"
Psalm 90:14-17 (NLT)

"When you face stormy seas I will be there with
you with endurance and calm; you will not be
engulfed in raging rivers.
 If it seems like you're walking through fire with
flames licking at your limbs, keep going; you won't
be burned." Isaiah 43:2 (The Voice)

"The Lord God is my strength [my source of courage, my invincible army]; He has made my feet [steady and sure] like hinds' feet And makes me walk [forward with spiritual confidence] on my high places [of challenge and responsibility]."
Habakkuk 3:19 (AMP)

"The LORD is the One who goes ahead of you; He will be with you He will not fail you or forsake you. Do not fear or be dismayed."
Deuteronomy 31:8 (NASB)

"Be strong. Take courage... God is striding ahead of you. He's right there with you. He won't let you down; He won't leave you. Don't be intimidated. Don't worry." Deuteronomy 31:8 (MSG)

*"Yet this I call to mind
    and therefore I have hope:
Because of the Lord's great love [I am] not consumed,
    for His compassions never fail.
They are new every morning;
    great is Your faithfulness.
I say to myself, 'The Lord is my portion;
    therefore I will wait for Him.'"*
Lamentations 3:21-24 (NIV)

"…I say to myself, 'The Lord is everything I will ever need.
   So I will put my hope in Him.'"
Lamentations 3:24 (NIRV)

⌒

"I will go before you and make the rough places smooth…"
Isaiah 45:2 (NASB)

⌒

"The eternal God is your refuge,
   and His everlasting arms are under you."
Deuteronomy 33:27 (NLT)

⌒

"Consider it a sheer gift, friends, when tests and challenges come at you from all sides. You know that under pressure, your faith-life is forced into the open and shows its true colors. So don't try to get out of anything prematurely. Let it do its work so you become mature and well-developed, not deficient in any way." James 1:2-4 (MSG)

⌒

"The Lord also will be a refuge and a stronghold for the oppressed,
A refuge in times of trouble;
And those who know Your name [who have experienced Your precious mercy] will put their confident trust in You,
For You, O Lord, have not abandoned those who seek You."
Psalm 9:9-10 (AMP)

"'For I,' declares the Lord, 'will be a wall of fire around her [protecting her from enemies], and I will be the glory in her midst.'"
Zechariah 2:5 (AMP)

"I can do all things [which He has called me to do] through Him who strengthens and empowers me [to fulfill His purpose—I am self-sufficient in Christ's sufficiency; I am ready for anything and equal to anything through Him who infuses me with inner strength and confident peace.]"
Philippians 4:13 (AMP)

"Do not, therefore, fling away your [fearless] confidence, for it has a glorious and great reward. For you have need of patient endurance [to bear up under difficult circumstances without compromising], so that when you have carried out the will of God, you may receive and enjoy to the full what is promised."
Hebrews 10:35-36 (AMP)

"So do not throw away this confident trust in the Lord. Remember the great reward it brings you! Patient endurance is what you need now, so that you will continue to do God's will. Then you will receive all that He has promised."
Hebrews 10:35-36 (NLT)

"Because [she] holds fast to me in love, I will deliver [her];
I will protect [her], because [she] knows my name.
When [she] calls to me, I will answer [her];
I will be with [her] in trouble;
I will rescue [her] and honor [her].
With long life I will satisfy [her]
and show [her] my salvation."
Psalm 91:14-16 (ESV)

"I waited patiently for the Lord to help me,
and He... heard my cry...
He set my feet on solid ground
and steadied me as I walked along.
He has given me a new song to sing,
a hymn of praise to our God.
Many will see what He has done and be amazed.
They will put their trust in the Lord."
Psalm 40:1-3 (NLT)

"Are not two sparrows sold for a penny? Yet not one
of them will fall to the ground outside your Father's
care... You, beloved, are worth so much more than
a whole flock of sparrows. God knows everything
about you, even the number of hairs on your head.
So do not fear."
Matthew 10:29-31 (NIV, The Voice)

"He gives His beloved sleep."
Psalm 127:2 (NKJV)

"... letting the Spirit control your mind leads to life
and peace."
Romans 8:6 (NLT)

"God is our shelter and our strength.
    When troubles seem near, God is nearer, and He's
ready to help."
Psalm 46:1 (The Voice)

"The Eternal will finish what He started in me.
    Your faithful love, O Eternal One, lasts forever..."
Psalm 138:8 (The Voice)

"But He knows every detail of what is happening
to me; and when He has examined me, He will
pronounce me... as pure as solid gold."
Job 23:10 (TLB)

"...live with the confidence that there is nothing in
the universe with the power to separate us from
God's love... His love will triumph over death,
life's troubles, fallen angels, or dark rulers in the
heavens. There is nothing in our present or future
circumstances that can weaken His love. There
is no power above us or beneath us—no power
that could ever be found in the universe that can
distance us from God's passionate love, which
is lavished upon us through our Lord Jesus, the
Anointed One!" Romans 8:38-39 (TPT)

"You [oh God] have surrounded me on every side, behind me and before me, and You have placed Your hand gently on my shoulder.
It is the most amazing feeling to know how deeply You know me, inside and out; the realization of it is so great that I cannot comprehend it."
Psalm 139:5-6 (The Voice)

"... casting all your cares [all your anxieties, all your worries, and all your concerns, once and for all] on Him, for He cares about you [with deepest affection, and watches over you very carefully]."
1 Peter 5:7 (AMP)

"Those who hope in Me will not be disappointed."
Isaiah 49:23 (NIV)

"You are safe with Me, for My power is great and absolute. My understanding is unlimited."
Psalm 147:5 (TLB)

"Hold tightly to Me, for I have promised to never leave you and I am reliable and trustworthy and faithful to My word..." Hebrews 10:23-24 (AMP)

"You will keep him in perfect peace,
Whose mind is stayed on You,
Because he trusts in You."
Isaiah 26:3 (NKJV)

"You will keep in perfect and constant peace the one
whose mind is steadfast [that is, committed and
focused on You—in both inclination and character],
Because he trusts and takes refuge in You [with
hope and confident expectation]."
Isaiah 26:3 (AMP)

⌒

"My grace is sufficient for you, for My power is
made perfect in weakness."
2 Corinthians 12:9 (NIV)

"My grace is sufficient for you [My loving
kindness and My mercy are more than
enough—always available—regardless of the
situation]; for [My] power is being perfected [and
is completed and shows itself most effectively] in
[your] weakness."
2 Corinthians 12:9 (AMP)

⌒

"When anxiety was great within me, Your
consolation brought me joy." Psalm 94:19 (NIV)

⌒

*"The Lord is my strength and my [impenetrable]
shield; My heart trusts [with unwavering
confidence] in Him, and I am helped;
Therefore my heart greatly rejoices..."*
Psalm 28:7 (AMP)

*"But You, Eternal One, wrap around me like
an impenetrable shield.
... You are my glory, the One who holds my head
high."* Psalm 3:3 (The Voice, NLT)

*"May your roots go down deep into the soil of God's
marvellous love; and may you be able to feel and
understand, as all God's children should, how long,
how wide, how deep, and how high His love really
is; and to experience this love for yourselves, though
it is so great that you will never see the end of it or
fully know or understand it. And so at last you will
be filled up with God Himself."*
Ephesians 3:17-19 (TLB)

*"The Lord your God is with you... He will take great
delight in you, He will quiet you with His love..."*
Zephaniah 3:17 (NIV)

"... casting all your cares [all your anxieties, all your worries, and all your concerns, once and for all] on Him, for He cares about you [with deepest affection, and watches over you very carefully]."
1 Peter 5:7 (AMP)

"The LORD is good to those whose hope is in Him, to the one who seeks Him..." Lamentations 3:25 (NIV)

"I will be your God throughout your lifetime—
   until your hair is white with age.
I made you, and I will care for you.
   I will carry you along and save you."
Isaiah 46:4 (NLT)

"I have loved you with an everlasting love—
   out of faithfulness I have drawn you close."
Jeremiah 31:3 (The Voice)

"The Lord your God is with you... He will take great delight in you, He will QUIET YOU with His love..."
Zephaniah 3:17 (NIV)

"...You will REST in His love"
Zephaniah 3:17 (NCV)

"...He will RENEW you with His love"
Zephaniah 3:17 (MEV)

"...He will CALM all your fears"
Zephaniah 3:17 (NLT)

"...He will REFRESH your life with His love"
Zephaniah 3:17 (CEV)

"... He is the Champion who will rescue you."
Zephaniah 3:17 (The Voice)

"Jesus Christ is the same yesterday, today, and forever." Hebrews 13:8 (NKJV)

Part Two

God's Words of Life
for a Healing Journey

"He was wounded for our transgressions,
He was bruised for our iniquities;
The chastisement for our peace was upon Him,
And by His stripes we are healed."
Isaiah 53:5 (NKJV)

"... the injuries He suffered became our healing."
Isaiah 53:5 (The Voice)

"... we are healed because of His wounds."
Isaiah 53:5 (NCV)

∽

"He heals the broken-hearted
And binds up their wounds [healing their pain and
comforting their sorrow]." Psalm 147:3 (AMP)

∽

"The Eternal is my shepherd, He cares for me always. He provides me rest in rich, green fields beside streams of refreshing water. He soothes my fears; He makes me whole again, steering me off worn, hard paths to roads where truth and righteousness echo His name. Even in the unending shadows of death's darkness, I am not overcome by fear. Because You are with me in those dark moments, near with Your protection and guidance, I am comforted. You spread out a table before me, provisions in the midst of attack from my enemies; You care for all my needs, anointing my head with soothing, fragrant oil, filling my cup again and again with Your grace. Certainly Your faithful protection and loving provision will pursue me where I go, always, everywhere. I will always be with the Eternal, in Your house forever."
Psalm 23 (The Voice)

"Listen carefully, my dear child, to everything that I teach you,
and pay attention to all that I have to say.
Fill your thoughts with my words
until they penetrate deep into your spirit.
Then, as you unwrap my words,
they will impart true life and radiant health
into the very core of your being."
Proverbs 4:20-22 (TPT)

"Let them penetrate deep into your heart,
for they bring life to those who find them,
and healing to their whole body."
Proverbs 4:20-22 (NLT)

◦∽

"I will give rest to those who are tired. I will satisfy
those who are weak."
Jeremiah 31:25 (NIRV)

◦∽

"On the day I called, You answered me;
And You made me bold and confident with
[renewed] strength in my life."
Psalm 138:3 (AMP)

◦∽

"My grace is sufficient for you, for My power is
made perfect in weakness."
2 Corinthians 12:9 (NIV)

"My grace is sufficient for you [My loving
kindness and My mercy are more than
enough—always available—regardless of the
situation]; for [My] power is being perfected [and
is completed and shows itself most effectively] in
[your] weakness."
2 Corinthians 12:9 (AMP)

◦∽

"O Lord my God,
I cried to You for help, and You have healed me."
Psalm 30:2 (AMP)

"... and You restored my health."
Psalm 30:2 (NLT)

⌒◡

"The Lord will guide you continually, and satisfy
your soul in drought, and strengthen your bones;
you shall be like a watered garden, and like a
spring of water, whose waters do not fail."
Isaiah 58:11 (NKJV)

"The LORD will guide you continually, giving
you water when you are dry and restoring your
strength. You will be like a well-watered garden,
like an ever-flowing spring."
Isaiah 58:11 (NLT)

⌒◡

"I have heard your prayer and seen your tears. I
will heal you."
2 Kings 20:5 (NLT)

⌒◡

"But the Lord stood with me and strengthened me."
2 Timothy 4:17 (NASB)

⌒◡

"Heal me, Lord, and I will be healed;
  save me and I will be saved,
  for You are the One I praise."
Jeremiah 17:14 (NIV)

⌒

"O Lord my God, I cried to You for help, and You have healed me."
Psalm 30:2 (AMP)

⌒

"For you made the Eternal [your] refuge,
  the Most High your only home.
No evil will come to you;
  plagues will be turned away at your door."
Psalm 91:9-10 (The Voice)

⌒

"Because [she] clings to Me in love,
  I will rescue [her] from harm;
  I will set [her] above danger.
Because [she] has known Me by name,
[She] will call on Me, and I will answer.
  I'll be with [her] through hard times;
  I'll rescue [her] and grant [her] honour.
I'll reward [her] with many good years on this earth and let [her] witness My salvation."
Psalm 91:14-16 (The Voice)

⌒

215

*"For You have rescued my life from death,
My eyes from tears, And my feet from
stumbling and falling. I will walk [in submissive
wonder] before the Lord In the land of the living."*
Psalm 116:8-9 (AMP)

∽

*"He heals the broken-hearted and binds up their
wounds [healing their pain and comforting their
sorrow]."* Psalm 147:3 (AMP)

∽

*"I know the Lord is always with me.
    I will not be shaken, for He is right beside me.
No wonder my heart is glad, and I rejoice.
    My body rests in safety."*
Psalm 16:8-9 (NLT)

∽

*"He sends forth His word and heals them; He
rescues them from the grave."*
Psalm 107:20 (NLT)

∽

*"Worship the Lord your God and His blessing will
be on your food and water. I will take sickness
away from among you."* Exodus 23:25 (NIV)

∽

"Heal me, o Lord - and I shall be healed. Save me, and I shall be saved - for You are my praise." Jeremiah 17:14 (NIV)

"Praise the Lord, O my soul, and forget not all His benefits - Who forgives all your sins and heals all your diseases." Psalm 103:2-3 (NIV)

"And if the Spirit of Him who raised Jesus from the dead is living in you - He who raised Christ from the dead will also give life to your mortal bodies through His Spirit who lives in you." Romans 8:11 (NLT)

"He took up our infirmities and carried our diseases." Matthew 8:17 (GNT)

"He Himself bore our sins in His body on the tree - so that we might die to sins and live for righteousness. By His wounds I have been healed." 1 Peter 2:24 (NLT)

"Whatever they plot against the Lord, He will bring to an end. Affliction will not come a second time." Nahum 1:9 (NKJV)

"With long life will I satisfy her and show her my salvation." Psalm 91:16 (NKJV)

"The Lord will keep you free from every disease." Deuteronomy 7:15 (NIV)

"I have heard your prayer. I have seen your tears. And I will heal you." 2 Kings 20:5 (NIRV)

"And so Jesus went throughout Galilee. He taught in the synagogues. He preached the good news of the Kingdom, and He healed people, ridding their bodies of sickness and disease. Word spread all over Syria, as more and more sick people came to Him. The innumerable ill who came before Him had all sorts of diseases, they were in crippling pain; they were possessed by demons; they had seizures; they were paralyzed. But Jesus healed them all." Matthew 4:23-24 (The Voice)

"When evening came, they brought to Him many who were under the power of demons; and He cast out the evil spirits with a word, and restored to health all who were sick [exhibiting His authority as Messiah], so that He fulfilled what was spoken by the prophet Isaiah: "He Himself took our infirmities [upon Himself] and carried away our diseases." Matthew 8:16-17 (AMP)

"Then a woman who had suffered from a hemorrhage for twelve years came up behind Him and touched the [tassel] fringe of His outer robe; for she had been saying to herself, "If I only touch His outer robe, I will be healed." But Jesus turning and seeing her said, "Take courage, daughter; your [personal trust and confident] faith [in Me] has made you well." And at once the woman was [completely] healed."
Matthew 9:20-22 (AMP)

"'But I will restore you to health and heal your wounds', declares the Lord."
Jeremiah 30:17 (NIV)

"I will not die but live, and will proclaim what the Lord has done."
Psalm 118:17 (NIV)

～

"He heals all my diseases."
Psalm 103:3 (NLT)

～

"O Lord my God - I cried to You and You have healed me." Psalm 30:2 (NLT)

～

How To Know Jesus Personally

If you have never taken the step of faith to surrender your life to Jesus, I can think of no better way to end this book than to give you that opportunity. Here are a few simple truths to understand...

1. God loves you and has an exciting plan for your life. The Bible says, *"This is how much God loved the world: He gave His Son, His one and only Son. And this is why: so that no one need be destroyed; by believing in Him, anyone can have a whole and lasting life."* John 3:16 (MSG)

2. People are sinful and separated from God. The Bible says that everyone has sinned; we all fall short of God's standard. The result of sin is spiritual death, which is separation from God (Romans 3:23, 6:23).

3. God sent His Son to die for your sins. Jesus died to take our punishment, so we could have a relationship with God and be with Him forever. *"God showed His great love for us by sending Christ to die for us while we were still sinners."* (Romans 5:8). Jesus is the only way to God. He said, *"I am the way, and the truth, and the life; no one comes to the Father, but through Me"* (John 14:6).

4. You can receive God's forgiveness today! We can't earn salvation; we are saved by God's grace when we have faith in His Son, Jesus Christ. All you have to do is believe you are a sinner, that Christ died for your sins, and ask His forgiveness. Then turn from your sins (that's called repentance). Jesus knows you and loves you. What matters to Him is the attitude of your heart...your honesty.

Here is the best "prayer starter" I could ever give you... a prayer of faith to receive Jesus into your life...

> *Dear God, I realize that I'm*
> *a sinner, and I ask for Your*
> *forgiveness. I believe Jesus Christ*
> *is Your Son. I believe that He died*
> *for my sins and that You raised*
> *Him to life. I now trust Him as my*
> *Saviour and follow Him as Lord of*
> *my life. Guide my life and help me*
> *to do your will. I pray this in the*
> *name of Jesus. Amen.*

If you prayed that prayer, CONGRATULATIONS! I encourage you to tell someone whom you believe will be excited to hear this news. Find a Bible-based church in your area, and connect with others who can help you grow in your new journey with Jesus. Spend time daily with Him... perhaps having "Coffee with Him"... reading the Bible and talking to Him in prayer.

May God bless you,
Ann

Made in the USA
Middletown, DE
08 July 2020

12295890R00137